Individual Book Report Forms

P9-CKU-827

Real or Make-Believe?

Individual Book Report Form

Literature Skill Focus: Determining if a story is fiction or nonfiction

1. Reading at School

- Read a nonfiction book such as *Scarecrows* by Lola M. Schaefer to your class. Ask students if the things in the book might actually happen. Lead them to the conclusion that the photographs and descriptions of scarecrows indicate it is a true story. Tell them that the story is real, or nonfiction.

- Read a fiction book on the same topic, such as *Jeb Scarecrow's Pumpkin Patch,* to your class. In this story, Jeb Scarecrow plans how to protect his pumpkin patch from the pesky crows. Ask students if this story is real. Have them give specific examples from the story that support their opinions. Lead them to see that this book is make-believe. Tell them that the story is make-believe, or fiction.

2. Reading at Home

- Have students choose a real or make-believe book from the library. They take the book home to read independently or with parent help. Together, the parent and student complete the form on page 3. The student returns the form and the book to school.

3. Sharing the Book Reports

- Briefly review the differences between real and make-believe books. Display the two books you read.

- Invite students to share the title of the book they chose and to tell whether it was a real or make-believe story. Have them stack their book report forms on top of the appropriate model book.

- When all the students have shared their books, count to see how many real and how many make-believe books were read. Record the results.

Good Books to Read

Nonfiction

Chameleon, Chameleon by Joy Cowley

Destination: Australia by Jonathan Grupper

Henry David's House by Henry David Thoreau

Houses and Homes by Ann Morris

Meteors and Meteorites by Gregory Vogt

Scarecrows by Lola M. Schaefer

Fiction

A Color of His Own by Leo Lionni

Henry Builds a Cabin by Donald B. Johnson

A House Is a House for Me by Mary Ann Hoberman

Jeb Scarecrow's Pumpkin Patch by Jana Dillon

Meteor! by Patricia Polacco

Possum Magic by Mem Fox

Name_____

Real or
Make-Believe?
Book Report Form

Title:

Author:

Illustrator:

Was the story real or make-believe?   real   make-believe

How did you know?

Dear Parents,
This is your child's independent reading book. After your child has read the book, discuss whether the story is real or make-believe. Encourage your child to give reasons for his or her choice. Help your child fill in the report form.

This book report is due back in class: _____   Parent Signature _____

Could It Be Real?
Individual Book Report Form

Literature Skill Focus: Determining if a story is realistic

1. Reading at School

• Read *The Knight and the Dragon* by Tomie dePaola to your class. This is the story of a sheepish knight and an inexperienced dragon who prepare to fight each other. Ask students if the events and descriptions in the book might have actually happened. Have students give specific examples from the story that support their opinions. Lead them to see that this book is a make-believe story based on fantasy. It could not actually have happened.

• In contrast, read *Knights in Shining Armor* by Gail Gibbons to your class. This is a nonfiction book about knights who actually lived long ago. It includes information about armor, tournaments, chivalry, and the feudal system.

• Ask students if the events in this book could have happened. Again, ask them to give specific examples to support their opinions. Explain that if the events could actually happen, the story is realistic.

2. Reading at Home

• Have students choose a fiction or nonfiction book from the library. They take the book home to read independently or with parent help. Together, the student and parent complete the form on page 5. The student returns the form and the book to school.

3. Sharing the Book Reports

• Briefly review the term *realistic*. Display the two books you read to model the concept.

• Invite students to share the title of the book they chose and to tell if the story they read was realistic.

Good Books to Read

Fantasy

Everything I Know About Pirates by Tom Lichtenheld

The Knight and the Dragon by Tomie dePaola

Moki and the Magic Surfboard: A Hawaiian Fantasy by Bruce Hale

Realistic

Knights in Shining Armor by Gail Gibbons

Pirates: A Nonfiction Companion to Pirates Past Noon by Will Osborne

Why Do Snakes Hiss? And Other Questions About Snakes, Lizards, and Turtles by Joan Holub

I'm real.

Really?

Name_____

Could It Be Real?

Book Report Form

Title:

Author:

Illustrator:

Could the story be real?   yes   no

Tell why you think the story could be real.

Dear Parents,
This is your child's independent reading book. After your child has read the book, discuss if the story could be real. Encourage your child to support his or her opinion with examples from the story. Help your child fill in the report form.

This book report is due back in class: _____   Parent Signature _____

The Main Character
Individual Book Report Form

Literature Skill Focus: Identifying and describing the main character in a story

1. Reading at School
- Briefly review the term *character* with students. A character is a person, an animal, or an imaginary creature represented in a story. Explain that usually a book has one or two important, or main, characters.

- Read *Smoky Night* by Eve Bunting to your class. This book is a Caldecott Medal winner that was inspired by the Los Angeles riots. It is about cats and neighbors who couldn't get along until a smoky night brings them together.

- Have students draw the character they think is the main character and write a sentence about that character. Discuss your students' choices. Extend the discussion by asking if the characters would make good friends.

2. Reading at Home
- Have students choose a fiction book from the library. They take the book home to read independently or with parent help. Together, the student and parent complete the form on page 7. The student returns the form and the book to school.

3. Sharing the Book Reports
- Display student drawings of main characters on a bulletin board. Gather students around the bulletin board.

- Invite students to describe the main character in the book they read and to tell if they would like to have that character as a friend.

Good Books to Read

Airmail to the Moon by Tom Birdseye

Cross-Country Cat by Mary Calhoun

I Know a Lady by Charlotte Zolotow

Lilly's Purple Plastic Purse by Kevin Henkes

Miss Nelson Is Missing! by Harry Allard and James Marshall

Olivia by Ian Falconer

Psssst! It's Me...the Bogeyman by Barbara Park

Smoky Night by Eve Bunting

Tacky the Penguin by Helen Lester

Miss Nelson was my teacher. One day she went missing.

Name_____

person

Main Character
Book Report Form

animal

imaginary creature

Title:

Author:

Illustrator:

Draw the main character here.

Write a sentence that tells about the character.

_____

_____

Would you like to have the character as a friend?   yes   no
Tell why or why not.

_____

_____

The character is:

☐ a person   ☐ an imaginary creature   ☐ an animal

Dear Parents,
This is your child's independent reading book. After your child has read the book, ask him or her to tell you who is the main character of the story. Encourage your child to describe the character and to tell if the character would be a good friend. Help your child fill in the report form.

This book report is due back in class: _____   Parent Signature _____

Describe the Main Character

Individual Book Report Form

Literature Skill Focus: Describing the main character

1. Reading at School

- Briefly review the idea that there is often one character in a story that is most important. Explain that this character is called the main character. Discuss with students the different kinds of things they know about story characters—what they like to do, how they feel, what they look like, and how they treat others. List the categories students suggest on a chart.

- Then read *Tops and Bottoms* by Janet Stevens. Have students identify the main character. Is it Hare or Bear? Next to each category, write notes about the character. Use some of the recorded information to model a sentence that describes the character. For example, Bear loves to sleep in his favorite chair.

2. Reading at Home

- Have students choose a fiction book from the library. They take the book home to read independently or with parent help. Together, the student and parent complete the form on page 9. The student returns the form and the book to school.

3. Sharing the Book Reports

- Briefly review the many ways to describe a character. Invite students to share the title of the book they chose and to tell one thing about the main character.

Good Books to Read

Alexander and the Terrible, Horrible, No Good, Very Bad Day by Judith Viorst

Badly Drawn Dog by Emma Dodson

Hattie and the Wild Waves: A Story from Brooklyn by Barbara Cooney

I Dream of Trains by Angela Johnson

Prince Cinders by Babette Cole

Song and Dance Man by Karen Ackerman

Stellaluna by Janell Cannon

Tops and Bottoms by Janet Stevens

Unlovable by Dan Yaccarino

My favorite character is Dirty Harry. My pigtails look just like his ears.

Name_____

Describe the Main Character
Book Report Form

Title:

Author:

Illustrator:

Main Character:

Circle words that tell about the character.

shy	determined	hungry
brave	weak	mean
gentle	silly	kind
rough	serious	old
strong	hardworking	tired
sick	smart	busy

Dear Parents,
This is your child's independent reading book. After your child has read the book, discuss the main character. Together, think of words that describe how the character looks and acts. Help your child fill in the report form.

This book report is due back in class: _____   Parent Signature _____

Cast of Characters

Individual Book Report Form

Literature Skill Focus: Identifying story characters and choosing the most important

1. Reading at School

- Ask students to brainstorm a definition of *characters*. For example, characters are the people and animals in a story. Explain that all of the characters together are sometimes called the cast of characters.

- Read *Max's Dragon Shirt* by Rosemary Wells. In this story, Max and his sister Ruby go to a department store with five dollars. They are supposed to replace Max's overalls, but Max insists on buying a dragon shirt instead. Ask students to name the characters. Record them. The characters are Max, Ruby, a teenager, the perfume lady, the saleslady, and the policemen.

- Model a description of the cast of characters. For example, the characters in *Max's Dragon Shirt* include a brother, Max and his sister Ruby, and all the people they meet on a shopping trip. Have students tell one thing each character did in the story. Ask students which character is the most important.

2. Reading at Home

- Have students choose a fiction book from the library. They take the book home to read independently or with parent help. Together, the student and parent complete the form on page 11. The student returns the form and the book to school.

3. Sharing the Book Reports

- Review the term *cast of characters*. Invite students to share the title of the book they read and to name a few of the characters in the cast.

Good Books to Read

Auntie Claus by Elise Primavera

The Funny Little Woman by Arlene Mosel

Max's Dragon Shirt by Rosemary Wells

Mirette on the High Wire by Emily Arnold McCully

Nana Upstairs & Nana Downstairs by Tomie dePaola

Saving Sweetness by Diane Stanley

The Three Little Javelinas by Susan Lowell

The War Between the Vowels and the Consonants by Priscilla Turner

I am the main one!

That's what he thinks!

Name_____

Cast of Characters
Book Report Form

Draw the cast of characters.
Write the name of each one.

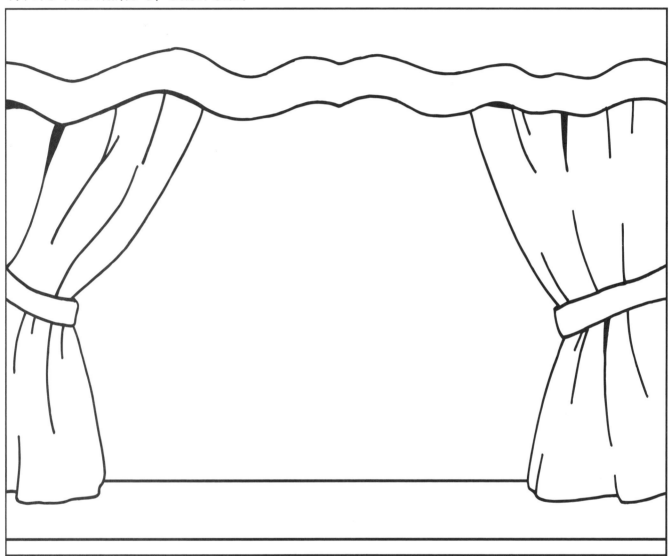

Circle the most important character.
Write a sentence that tells what that character does.

_____

_____

Dear Parents,
This is your child's independent reading book. After your child has read the book, make a list of the characters in the book. Discuss which character is the most important. Encourage your child to give reasons for his or her choice. Help your child fill in the report form.

This book report is due back in class: _____   Parent Signature _____

On Location

Individual Book Report Form

Literature Skill Focus: Identifying the location of a story

1. Reading at School

• Introduce the term *setting* to your students. Explain that the setting of a story is the place and time a story occurs. Today, you will be focusing on the place.

• As you read *Hush!* by Minfong Ho, ask students to listen for clues to the location. Some of the clues are jungle-like, buildings on stilts, rice barn, monkey in tree, elephant, mother's clothes, baby's hammock. The dedication and subtitle of the book also identify the location. The location is on a farm in Thailand.

2. Reading at Home

• Have students choose a fiction book from the library. They take the book home to read independently or with parent help. Together, the student and parent complete the form on page 13. The student returns the form and the book to school.

3. Sharing the Book Reports

• Prepare several general labels—"in the United States," "in another country," "in outer space." You may need to make additional labels during the sharing time.

• Invite each student to share the title of the book he or she chose. Have students tell where the story happened and give several clues that helped them determine the location. Place the completed book report form next to the label that tells where the story happened.

• When all students have reported on their books, look at the graph they created and draw some conclusions about where the stories took place.

Good Books to Read

All the Places to Love by Patricia MacLachlan

Cloudy with a Chance of Meatballs by Judy Barrett

Gila Monsters Meet You at the Airport by Marjorie Weinman Sharmat

Hush! A Thai Lullaby by Minfong Ho

In November by Cynthia Rylant

Ox-Cart Man by Donald Hall

Round Trip by Ann Jonas

Time Train by Paul Fleischman

Where the River Begins by Thomas Locker

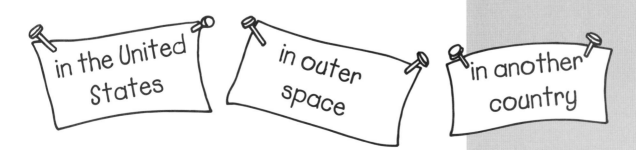

Name_____

On Location
Book Report Form

Title:

Author:

Illustrator:

Some clues to the story location:

Where the story takes place:

Dear Parents,

This is your child's independent reading book. After your child has read the book, discuss where the story takes place. Together, find some clues that help identify the location. Help your child fill in the report form.

This book report is due back in class: _____   Parent Signature _____

Location, Location, Location

Individual Book Report Form

Literature Skill Focus: Identifying where the story takes place and its importance to the story

1. Reading at School

- Review the term *setting*. Tell students that setting includes two things: where the story takes place and when it takes place. This lesson focuses on the "where" part.

- Read *A Garden for a Groundhog* by Lorna Balian and *City Green* by DyAnne DiSalvo-Ryan. Compare the settings of the two stories. The first story takes place in the country. The second takes place in the city.

- Ask students to think about whether the settings were important to the stories. For example, would Mrs. O'Leary's story have been the same if it had taken place in a busy city?

2. Reading at Home

- Have students choose a fiction book from the library. They take the book home to read independently or with parent help. Together, the student and parent complete the form on page 15. The student returns the form and the book to school.

3. Sharing the Book Reports

- Invite students to share the title of the book they read and to tell where the story took place and if the location was important to the story.

- Tally the responses to the setting's importance in two categories: "Important to story" (the story would have changed significantly if the setting changed); "Unimportant to story" (the story could have taken place in a different location without significantly changing).

Good Books to Read

The Best Town in the World by Byrd Baylor

City Green by DyAnne DiSalvo-Ryan

Diary of a Worm by Doreen Cronin

A Garden for a Groundhog by Lorna Balian

Hershel and the Hanukkah Goblins by Eric Kimmel

Hill of Fire by Thomas P. Lewis

The Little House by Virginia Lee Burton

Lost by Paul Brett Johnson and Celeste Lewis

The Man Who Walked Between the Towers by Mordicai Gerstein

Stella Louella's Runaway Book by Lisa Campbell Ernst

Name_____

Location, Location, Location

Book Report Form

city • neighborhood • country • forest

Title:

Author:

Illustrator:

Where did the story take place?

Write three clues to the location.

Dear Parents,

This is your child's independent reading book. After your child has read the book, discuss where the story takes place. Together, find some clues that help identify the location. Help your child fill in the report form.

This book report is due back in class: _____   Parent Signature _____

First, Next, and Last

Individual Book Report Form

Literature Skill Focus: Sequencing story events

1. Reading at School

- Write the words *first, next,* and *last* on a chart. Ask students to listen to find out what happens first, next, and last in the story you read.

- Read *Beardream* by Will Hobbs. Have students retell the story by telling what happened first, next, and last.

  First: Spring arrives and the Great Bear hasn't been seen by the villagers.

  Next: Short Tail decides to climb the mountain and find Great Bear. He falls asleep after the hard climb and has a dream.

  Last: Short Tail returns to the village and shares his dream with the villagers.

2. Reading at Home

- Have students choose a fiction book from the library. They take the book home to read independently or with parent help. Together, the student and parent complete the form on page 17. The student returns the form and the book to school.

3. Sharing the Book Reports

- Briefly review the idea of retelling a story by reporting what happened first, next, and last.

- Invite a few students to share the title of the book they read and to retell the story.

Good Books to Read

Beardream by Will Hobbs

The Doorbell Rang by Pat Hutchins

How to Make an Apple Pie and See the World by Marjorie Priceman

If You Take a Mouse to School by Laura Numeroff

Joseph Had a Little Overcoat by Simms Taback

The Keeping Quilt by Patricia Polacco

Pancakes, Pancakes! by Eric Carle

Pierre: A Cautionary Tale by Maurice Sendak

The Sweet Touch by Lorna Balian

 first

 next

 last

How to Report on Books • EMC 6008 • © Evan-Moor Corp.

Name_____

First, Next, and Last
Book Report Form

Title:

Author:

Illustrator:

What Happened?

First:

Next:

Last:

Dear Parents,
This is your child's independent reading book. After your child has read the book, ask him or her to retell the story. Help your child sequence the events by telling what happened first, next, and last. Together, fill in the report form.

This book report is due back in class: _____   Parent Signature _____

Problem and Solution

Individual Book Report Form

Literature Skill Focus: Identifying the problem and solution

1. Reading at School
- Read *The Secret Remedy Book* by Karin Cates. Ask students to identify the problem in the story and how it was solved. The problem is homesickness. Seven different remedies were suggested by the adult in the story. Ask the students to think about times when they have been homesick. List other solutions to homesickness.

2. Reading at Home
- Have students choose a fiction book from the library. They take the book home to read independently or with parent help. Together, the student and parent complete the form on page 19. The student returns the form and the book to school.

3. Sharing the Book Reports
- Invite students to share the title of the book they chose and to tell about the problem in the book. Record the results.

- When all students have completed their oral reports, discuss if any of the problems were similar.

Good Books to Read

Alexander and the Terrible, Horrible, No Good, Very Bad Day by Judith Viorst

A Chair for My Mother by Vera B. Williams

Harry and the Terrible Whatzit by Dick Gackenbach

Ira Sleeps Over by Bernard Waber

Kitten's First Full Moon by Kevin Henkes

The Secret Remedy Book: A Story of Comfort and Love by Karin Cates

This book is about a dog who loves baths!

FIDO

That is a problem.

Name_____

Problem and Solution
Book Report Form

Title:

Author: | Illustrator:

A problem faced by a character in the book:

This is how the problem was solved:

I would have solved the problem by:

I have the solution!

Dear Parents,
This is your child's independent reading book. After your child has read the book, discuss if there was a problem in the book and how it was solved. Ask your child if he or she would have solved the problem in the same way. Help your child fill in the report form.

This book report is due back in class: _____   Parent Signature _____

Here's What Happened

Individual Book Report Form

Literature Skill Focus: Retelling the story

1. Reading at School
- Write the words *First, Next,* and *Last* on a chart. Ask students to listen to find out what happens first, next, and last in the story you read.
- Read *"Let's Get a Pup!" Said Kate* by Bob Graham. Have students retell the story by telling what happens first, what happens next, and what happens last. First, Kate said, "Let's get a pup!" Next, the family went to the shelter. They took home an adorable puppy. Last, they went back to the shelter to get an older dog, as well.

2. Reading at Home
- Have students choose a fiction book from the library. They take the book home to read independently or with parent help. Together, the student and parent complete the form on page 21. The student returns the form and the book to school.

3. Sharing the Book Reports
- Schedule several book reports a day over a week-long period. Invite students to give a book talk that includes the title and author of the book and a short retelling.

Good Books to Read

Arthur's TV Trouble by Marc Brown

"Let's Get a Pup!" Said Kate by Bob Graham

The Mysterious Tadpole by Steven Kellogg

No Jumping on the Bed! by Tedd Arnold

The Stupids Step Out by Harry Allard

Well, first he lived in the jungle. But in the end, he learned to live in the city.

Funny Monkey

Name_____

Here's What Happened
Book Report Form

Title:	
Author:	Illustrator:

First:	Next:	Last:

The most important part of the book was _____

_____

_____

_____

_____

Dear Parents,
This is your child's independent reading book. After your child has read the book, have him or her retell the story. Help your child sequence the events by telling what happened first, next, and last. Fill in the report form with your child.

This book report is due back in class: _____ Parent Signature _____

That's the End of It!
Individual Book Report Form

Literature Skill Focus: Retelling the story ending

1. Reading at School
- Ask students to tell you what an ending is. Read *Swimmy* by Leo Lionni to your class.

- Have students draw pictures that show the ending of the story. Then ask several students to tell about their drawings.

- Restate the ending of the story in a summary sentence. For example, Swimmy taught the fish how to swim together like one giant fish, and together they chased away the big fish. Ask students whether they liked the ending or not. Have them support their choice by telling why.

2. Reading at Home
- Have students choose a fiction book from the library. They take the book home to read independently or with parent help. Together, the student and parent complete the form on page 23. The student returns the form and the book to school.

3. Sharing the Book Reports
- Invite students to share the title of the book they chose and to retell the story's ending. Ask students to tell whether they liked the ending and why.

Good Books to Read

The Biggest Frog in Australia by Susan L. Roth

Drummer Hoff by Barbara Emberley

The Great White Man-Eating Shark by Margaret Mahy

Harold and the Purple Crayon by Crockett Johnson

I Know an Old Lady Who Swallowed a Fly by Nadine Westcott

The Island of the Skog by Steven Kellogg

Leo the Late Bloomer by Robert Kraus

The Napping House by Audrey Wood

Swimmy by Leo Lionni

I read the Lion and the Mouse. I love the way they became friends in the end.

Name_____

That's the End of It!
Book Report Form

Title:

Author:

Illustrator:

Did you guess the ending?

yes   no

Did you like the ending?

yes   no

Tell why or why not.

Draw a picture to show the ending of the story.

Write a sentence that tells about the picture.

Dear Parents,
This is your child's independent reading book. After your child has read the book, discuss the story ending. Ask if your child thought the ending was a good one and why or why not. Help your child fill in the report form.

This book report is due back in class: _____   Parent Signature _____

Change the Ending
Individual Book Report Form

Literature Skill Focus: Thinking of an alternate ending

1. Reading at School
- Read *Raven: A Trickster Tale from the Pacific Northwest* by Gerald McDermott. Have students retell the ending of the story. For example, Raven changes back into a bird and flies off with the sun.

- Have students think of other endings that storytellers might have used to end this tale. For example, Raven flew off with the sun, but he dropped it and night came. Or, Raven tried to change back into a bird, and the Sky Chief's daughter put him in a cage.

2. Reading at Home
- Have students choose a fiction book from the library. They take the book home to read independently or with parent help. Together, the student and parent complete the form on page 25. The student returns the form and the book to school.

3. Sharing the Book Reports
- Invite students to share the title of the book they chose and to tell how the story ended. Then have them suggest one new ending for the story. You may need to allow several share-and-tell sessions for this activity.

Good Books to Read

Alistair in Outer Space by Marilyn Sadler

Axle Annie by Robin Pulver

Dog Breath: The Horrible Trouble with Hally Tosis by Dav Pilkey

Fix-it by David McPhail

The Giving Tree by Shel Silverstein

Imogene's Antlers by David Small

Pete's a Pizza by William Steig

Raven: A Trickster Tale from the Pacific Northwest by Gerald McDermott

Tikki Tikki Tembo by Arlene Mosel

The fact is, Goldilocks deserved to be punished!

Name_____

Change the Ending
Book Report Form

Change it, please!

Presto!

Title:

Author:

Illustrator:

The story ended this way:

Another way the story could end:

Dear Parents,
This is your child's independent reading book. After your child has read the book, discuss the story ending. Together, think of new ways the story might have ended. Help your child fill in the report form with one of the new endings.

This book report is due back in class: _____   Parent Signature _____

Gathering Facts

Individual Book Report Form

Literature Skill Focus: Identifying facts in fictional text

1. Reading at School

- Talk with students about what a fact is. A fact is a piece of information that is true, such as wombats live in Australia. Explain that even when a story is fiction, the author may include facts.

- Read *Diary of a Wombat* by Jackie French to your class. Ask the students to listen carefully to learn some facts about wombats.

- Have students recall the facts they have learned by listening to the story. For example, wombats are wild animals. Wombats like to eat grass, carrots, and oats. List the facts on a chart. If students are nonreaders, have them draw illustrations by each fact.

2. Reading at Home

- Students choose a fiction book from the library. They take the book home to read independently or with parent help. Together, the student and parent complete the form on page 27. The student returns the form and the book to school.

3. Sharing the Book Reports

- Briefly review with students what a fact is. Invite students to share the title of the book they read and one important fact they learned from the book.

Good Books to Read

A Cache of Jewels and Other Collective Nouns by Ruth Heller

Diary of a Wombat by Jackie French

How to Hide an Octopus and Other Sea Creatures by Ruth Heller

The Icky Bug Alphabet Book by Jerry Pallotta

Mailing May by Michael O. Tunnell

Officer Buckle and Gloria by Peggy Rathmann

A chicken lays 1 egg a day.

An egg takes 20 days to hatch.

Chickens

Name_____

Gathering Facts
Book Report Form

Even when a story is fiction, the author may include facts.

Title:	
Author:	Illustrator:
This book is about	

Write a fact you learned on each egg.

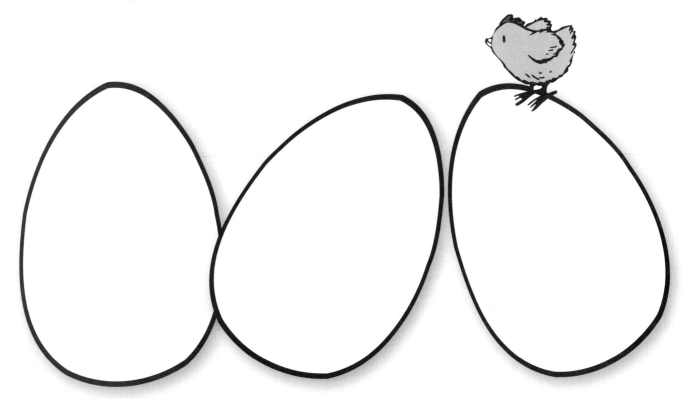

Dear Parents,
This is your child's independent reading book. After your child has read the book, discuss the information included in this fictional text. Help your child recall and list facts on the report form.

This book report is due back in class: _____   Parent Signature _____

Just the Facts
Individual Book Report Form

Literature Skill Focus: Identifying facts in nonfictional text

1. Reading at School
- Remind students that a fact is a piece of information that is true. Ask students to listen closely as you read *If You Hopped Like a Frog* by David Schwartz.
- Then have students recall a fact they learned by listening to the book. List their facts on a chart.

2. Reading at Home
- Students choose a nonfiction book from the library. They take the book home to read independently or with parent help. Together, the student and parent complete the form on page 29. The student returns the form and the book to school.

3. Sharing the Book Reports
- Invite students to share the title of the book they chose and an interesting fact they learned from reading it.

Good Books to Read

Chickens Aren't the Only Ones by Ruth Heller

If You Hopped Like a Frog by David Schwartz

The Kids' Cat Book by Tomie dePaola

Man on the Moon by Anastasia Suen

Red-Eyed Tree Frog by Joy Cowley

Seymour Simon's Book of Trains by Seymour Simon

Watch Me Grow—Duckling by Lisa Magloff

I learned how to tie knots.

I learned how to knit.

I learned about mice!

Name_____

Just the Facts
Book Report Form

I love to read!

I can learn lots of true information by reading.

Title:	
Author:	Illustrator:

Three facts that I learned:

1

2

3

* Put a star by the most important fact.

Dear Parents,
This is your child's independent reading book. After your child has read the book, discuss the factual information included. Help your child recall and list 3 facts on the report form. Finally, discuss which fact is the most important and star it.

This book report is due back in class: _____   Parent Signature _____

Introducing...the Author

Individual Book Report Form

Literature Skill Focus: Learning about a book's author

1. Reading at School
- Choose several books from your library that have author biographies on the book jackets.

- Share the books with your students. Show them where the information about the author is found. Explain that an author is the person who writes the words in a book. Read the information and discuss it.

2. Reading at Home
- Have students choose a book with an author biography from the library. They take the book home to read independently or with parent help. Together, the student and parent complete the form on page 31. The student returns the form and the book to school.

3. Sharing the Book Reports
- Have a chart ready to record the authors' names. Invite the students to share the title of the book they read, the name of the author, and one thing about the author.

- Ask students to notice if more than one book was written by the same author.

Leo Lionni

Frederick

Swimmy

Little Blue and
Little Yellow

Wow! He wrote a lot!

Good Books to Read

Eric Carle

Draw Me a Star

My Apron

Donald Crews

Bigmama's

Freight Train

Shortcut

Helen Lester

Author: A True Story

Hurty Feelings

Tomie dePaola

Now One Foot, Now the Other

Tom

Jon Scieszka and Lane Smith

Math Curse

The Stinky Cheese Man and Other Fairly Stupid Tales

Dr. Seuss

Daisy-Head Mayzie

Hooray for Diffendoofer Day!

My Many Colored Days

Janet Stevens

From Pictures to Words: A Book About Making a Book

Name_____

Introducing...the Author
Book Report Form

My favorite author is:

My favorite title is:

Where does the author live? _____

Has the author written other books?   yes   no

Name some of the books.

_____

_____

_____

Dear Parents,
This is your child's independent reading book. After your child has read the book, read together the information about the author. You may want to gather more information from the Internet or another source. Help your child fill in the report form.

This book report is due back in class: _____   Parent Signature _____

Introducing...the Illustrator

Individual Book Report Form

Literature Skill Focus: Learning about an illustrator

1. Reading at School

- Choose several books from your library that have illustrator biographies on the book jackets. (The Caldecott Medal winners are great selections.) Explain to students that the person who draws the pictures in a book is called the illustrator. Show them where information about the illustrator can be found.

- Show students the book *Brother Eagle, Sister Sky* by Susan Jeffers. Have students read the information about Susan Jeffers. Together, discuss how Miss Jeffers's drawings bring the words to life. For example, this book is based on the words of a Native American chief. He explains the web of life. The drawings portray a full circle, beginning with Native Americans living in harmony with nature, then depicting land stripped of its timber, and finally showing a Caucasian family replanting trees on barren land.

2. Reading at Home

- Have students choose a book that has an illustrator biography from the library. They take the book home to read independently or with parent help. Together, the student and parent complete the form on page 33. The student returns the form and the book to school.

3. Sharing the Book Reports

- Have a chart ready to record illustrators' names. Invite students to share the title of the book they read, the illustrator's name, and an interesting fact about the illustrator. Record the names as they are mentioned. Ask students to notice if more than one book was illustrated by the same person.

Good Books to Read

Jan Brett

Gingerbread Baby

On Noah's Ark

Marc Brown

Arthur's Nose

Arthur's Nose (25th Anniversary Edition)

Denise Fleming

Count!

In the Small, Small Pond

Susan Jeffers

Brother Eagle, Sister Sky

David Wiesner

Free Fall

The Three Pigs

I love Eric Carle's pictures.

Name_____

Introducing...the Illustrator
Book Report Form

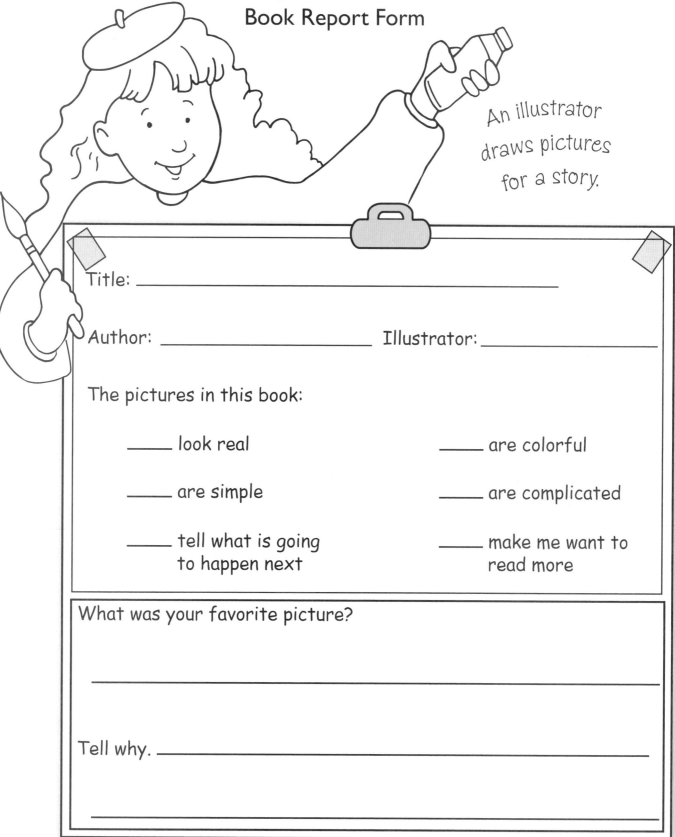

An illustrator draws pictures for a story.

Title: _____

Author: _____   Illustrator: _____

The pictures in this book:

_____ look real   _____ are colorful

_____ are simple   _____ are complicated

_____ tell what is going   _____ make me want to
      to happen next   read more

What was your favorite picture?

_____

Tell why. _____

_____

Dear Parents,
This is your child's independent reading book. After your child has read the book, discuss the illustrations. Talk about what they add to the story. Together, read the information about the illustrator on the book jacket. Help your child fill in the report form.

Find the Clues
Individual Book Report Form

Literature Skill Focus: Reading a mystery story

1. Reading at School
- Discuss with students what makes a *mystery*. For example, a mystery has a problem or a crime to solve, clues that lead to a solution, a wrongdoer, and a "detective" who solves the mystery.

- Read a simple mystery story to your students. Have them identify the problem, the clues, the wrongdoer, and the detective.

2. Reading at Home
- Have students choose a mystery story from the library. They take the book home to read independently or with parent help. Together, the student and parent complete the form on page 35. The student returns the form and the book to school.

3. Sharing the Book Reports
- Invite students to tell the title of the book they read and to tell what the problem or crime was. Ask them to keep the solution a secret for now.

Good Books to Read

Alphabet Mystery by Audrey Wood

Dot & Jabber and the Great Acorn Mystery by Ellen Stoll Walsh

Nate the Great and the Stolen Base and other *Nate the Great* books by Marjorie Weinman Sharmat

Schoolhouse Mystery by Gertrude Chandler Warner

Name_____

Find the Clues
Book Report Form

Title:

Author:

Illustrator:

Problem to be solved:

Clues:

The "Detective":

The Wrongdoer:

Dear Parents,
This is your child's independent reading book. After your child has read the book, discuss the ideas listed on the form.
Help your child fill in the information.

This book report is due back in class: _____   Parent Signature _____

Animals, Animals, Animals

Individual Book Report Form

Literature Skill Focus: Reading an animal story

1. Reading at School

- Explain to your class that animal stories may be about real animals in real or imaginary situations, or about imaginary animals in both kinds of situations. The characters are animals.

- Read *Seaman's Journal* by Patricia Reeder Eubank to your class. This is a journal written by Meriwether Lewis's Newfoundland dog as the dog accompanies Lewis and Clark on their historic expedition.

- Ask students if the story was about a real animal or an imaginary animal. The story is based on a real animal. Discuss whether the events in the story were real or imaginary. This story falls into the second category described below: "Real Animals—Imaginary Events."

2. Reading at Home

- Have students choose a book about animals from the library. They take the book home to read independently or with parent help. Together, the student and parent complete the form on page 37. The student returns the form and the book to school.

3. Sharing the Book Reports

- Create a grid with four columns like the one below.

- Invite students to share the title of the book they read and to classify it as one of the four types of animal stories. Encourage students to explain why they classified the book that way. List the titles on the chart.

Good Books to Read

Anansi and the Moss-Covered Rock by Eric Kimmel

Is Your Mama a Llama? by Deborah Guarino

Lost in the Woods: A Photographic Fantasy by Carl R. Sams II and Jean Stoick

Once There Was a Bull... (Frog) by Rick Walton

Seaman's Journal by Patricia Reeder Eubank

Somewhere in the Ocean by Jennifer Ward

Underwear! by Mary Elise Monsell

What Do You Do with a Kangaroo? by Mercer Mayer

Wild About Books by Judy Sierra

Real Animals Real Events	Real Animals Imaginary Events	Imaginary Animals Real Events	Imaginary Animals Imaginary Events

Name_____

Animals, Animals, Animals
Book Report Form

Title:

Author:	Illustrator:

What animal was the story about?

_____

Was the animal in the story real or imaginary?

_____

Were the events in the story real or imaginary?

_____

_____

_____

_____

_____

_____

Dear Parents,
This is your child's independent reading book. After your child has read the book, discuss the animals in the book. Have your child tell you if the animal is real or imaginary. Help your child fill in the report form.

This book report is due back in class: _____   Parent Signature _____

It Could Be Real!

Individual Book Report Form

Literature Skill Focus: Reading realistic fiction

1. Reading at School

- Discuss with your class the genre, or type of book, called *realistic fiction*. Realistic fiction is based on events that could really happen. Characters, settings, and details seem real. The stories are fiction. These stories often help us learn more about ourselves and other people.

- Read *Cleversticks* by Bernard Ashley to your class. This is the story of a Chinese-American boy who is unhappy at school because everyone else seems to be good at something. His teacher sees him using paintbrushes to pick up food. She encourages him to share his skill of using chopsticks with the others. Discuss whether the characters, settings, and details could be real.

2. Reading at Home

- Students choose a realistic fiction book from the library. They take the book home to read independently or with parent help. Together, the student and parent complete the form on page 39. The student returns the form and the book to school.

3. Sharing the Book Reports

- Briefly review the attributes of realistic fiction. Invite students to share the title of the book they read and to tell one thing in the story that was similar to something in their own lives.

Good Books to Read

The Art Lesson by Tomie dePaola

Cleversticks by Bernard Ashley

The Dot by Peter H. Reynolds

Our Teacher's Having a Baby by Eve Bunting

Silver Packages: An Appalachian Christmas Story by Cynthia Rylant

Uncle Jed's Barbershop by Margaree King Mitchell

What Are YOU So Grumpy About? by Tom Lichtenheld

Wilfrid Gordon McDonald Partridge by Mem Fox

The boy in the book caught the chickenpox just like me.

Sad Day

Name_____

It Could Be Real!
Book Report Form

I think it could be real.   Me, too.   *I like real stories.*

Title:

Author: Illustrator:

The characters in this story seemed real because

_____

_____

The setting in this story seemed real because

_____

_____

The events in this story seemed real because

_____

_____

Dear Parents,
This is your child's independent reading book. After your child has read the book, discuss whether the characters and events in the story were real or imaginary. Help your child fill in the report form.

This book report is due back in class: _____   Parent Signature _____

Fantastic!

Individual Book Report Form

Literature Skill Focus: Reading a fantasy story

1. Reading at School

- Introduce *fantasy* as a type of literature. Make-believe events and talking animals or objects are two important characteristics of fantasy stories. Fantasy stories frequently begin with the words "Once upon a time..." or "There once lived a...."

- Read *The Golden Sandal* by Rebecca Hickox to your class. In this story, there is a magic fish that saves the Cinderella character, a young Arabian girl.

- Have students identify the make-believe story events and characters in the story. Discuss any "magic" in the story.

2. Reading at Home

- Students choose a fantasy book from the library. They take the book home to read independently or with parent help. Together, the student and parent complete the form on page 41. The student returns the form and the book to school.

3. Sharing the Book Reports

- Create a chart with these headings: "Book Title," "Make-Believe Events," "Talking Animals and Objects."

- Fill in the chart as students share the fantasy books they have read.

- Display the chart so that students can use it to choose reading books and to write fantasy stories.

Good Books to Read

The Five Chinese Brothers by Claire Huchet Bishop and Kurt Wiese

The Golden Sandal: A Middle Eastern Cinderella Story by Rebecca Hickox

The Jolly Postman by Janet and Allan Ahlberg

Little Red Riding Hood by Trina Schart Hyman

Rumpelstiltskin by Paul O. Zelinsky

Sylvester and the Magic Pebble by William Steig

Book Title	Make-Believe Events	Talking Animals and Objects
Little Red Riding Hood	Wolf dresses like Grandma	Wolf

Once upon a time...

Name_____

Fantastic!
Book Report Form

I read a fantasy story.

Title:

Author: Illustrator:

Talking animals or objects in the story:

A magical event that happened in the story:

Dear Parents,
This is your child's independent reading book. After your child has read the book, discuss the talking animals or objects in the story. Talk about the magical events. Help your child fill in the report form.

This book report is due back in class: _____   Parent Signature _____

Parent Letter
Support Independent Reading

Dear Parents,

The most important thing you can do for a child is read with him or her. In addition, it is important that your child always have an independent reading book. Encourage your child's independent reading. Have your child read a part of the independent reading book to you. Discuss the story and the characters.

Throughout the year, I will be sending home book report forms and projects. Please support your child as he or she completes the assignment.

Thank you for your help. You are an important part of your child's learning team.

Sincerely,

Dear Parents,

The most important thing you can do for a child is read with him or her. In addition, it is important that your child always have an independent reading book. Encourage your child's independent reading. Have your child read a part of the independent reading book to you. Discuss the story and the characters.

Throughout the year, I will be sending home book report forms and projects. Please support your child as he or she completes the assignment.

Thank you for your help. You are an important part of your child's learning team.

Sincerely,

Individual Book Report Projects

A Character Stand-up

Individual Book Report Project

Literature Skill Focus: Identifying and describing the main character in a story

1. Teaching the Literature Skill

- Remind students that there is often one character in a story that is the most important. Explain that this character is called the main character.

- Read *Officer Buckle and Gloria* by Peggy Rathmann. Ask students to tell you the characters' names. List the characters on a chart. Have students choose the main character from the list, giving a reason for their choice. The main character could be either Officer Buckle or Gloria the dog.

- Finally, have students think of adjectives and phrases that describe the main character. Model writing a sentence using some of the students' ideas. For example, Gloria loved being the center of attention.

2. Modeling the Project

- Demonstrate how to make the character stand-up for *Officer Buckle and Gloria*.

3. Reading at Home

- Have students choose a fiction book from the library. They take home the book and their copy of the stand-up pattern on page 45.

- After reading the book, the student works with the parent to write a sentence that describes the character. Together, they make the stand-up. The student returns the book and the stand-up to school.

4. Sharing the Book Projects

- When the projects have been returned, display them, have a class discussion about the literature skill in the students' independent reading books, or have partners share their projects.

Character Stand-up

1. Write the title of the book and the names of the author and illustrator on the stand-up pattern.

2. Write a sentence that identifies and describes the main character.

3. Draw the main character on the form.

4. Color the character and cut out the stand-up form.

5. Roll the stand-up into a tube shape and tape the back to hold it together.

A Character Stand-up Book Report

Officer Buckle
character's name

Describe the main character:

How to Report on Books • EMC 6008 • © Evan-Moor Corp.

A Character Stand-up
Individual Book Report Project

1. Fill in the pattern.
2. Draw the character.
3. Cut out the stand-up and tape it into a tube shape.

Roll and tape here.

Describe the main character.

character's name

A Character Stand-up
A Book Report

Title:

Author:

Illustrator:

My Name:

A Book Cover

Individual Book Report Project

Literature Skill Focus: Designing a book cover

1. Teaching the Literature Skill

- Discuss with your class the information included on the cover of a book. Make a list of things your students think are most important. Discuss with them whether they are more likely to choose a book with a plain cover or an illustrated cover.

- Holding a plain paper over the cover, read *Mice and Beans* by Pam Muñoz Ryan. Ask students which character or event they would like to see on the cover.

- With the students, design a cover for the book. Be sure to include the title, the author, the illustrator, and an illustration of a story character or event.

2. Modeling the Project

- Demonstrate how to make the book cover for *Mice and Beans*. On a chart or a transparency copy of the form, write the book information.

3. Reading at Home

- Have students choose a book from the library. They take home the book, their copy of the cover pattern on page 47, and a sheet of 9" x 12" (23 x 30.5 cm) construction paper.

- After reading the book, the student works with the parent to create a new book cover. The student returns the book and the cover to school.

4. Sharing the Book Projects

- When the projects have been returned, display them, have a class discussion about the book covers that are especially appealing, or have partners share their projects.

Book Cover

1. Fold a 9" x 12" (23 x 30.5 cm) sheet of construction paper in half. On the outside, draw an illustration that represents a character or an event in the story. The illustration should invite a student to take the book off the shelf and begin to read.

2. Write the title of the book and the names of the author and illustrator on the cover. Use colorful lettering.

3. Cut out the form on page 47. Glue it inside the paper book cover.

Mice and Beans

by Pam Muñoz Ryan

Illustrated by Joe Cepeda

A Book Cover
Individual Book Report Project

1. Fold the construction paper in half to make a cover.
2. Draw a picture on the cover.
3. Write the title and the names of the author and the illustrator on the cover.
4. Glue the form to the inside of the cover.

The Characters:

I liked _____ best
      character's name

because

My Name:

A Book Report

My favorite part is:

A Book Mobile
Individual Book Report Project

Literature Skill Focus: Describing story characters

1. Teaching the Literature Skill

- Read *The Three Questions* by Jon J. Muth. With students' input, list the characters. Be sure to include animal and human characters. The characters are Nikolai, Sonya the heron, Gogol the monkey, Pushkin the dog, Leo the turtle, Panda, and Panda's child.

- Have students recall something they know about each character. Write a sentence describing each character next to that character's name. For example, a sentence that describes Nikolai is "Nikolai wanted to be a good person."

2. Modeling the Project

- Demonstrate how to make a book mobile for *The Three Questions*.

3. Reading at Home

- Have students choose a fiction book from the library. They take home the book and their copy of the mobile pattern on page 49.

- After reading the book, the student and parent make the book mobile. The student returns the book and the mobile to school.

4. Sharing the Book Projects

- When the projects have been returned, display them, have a class discussion about the literature skill in students' books, or have partners share their projects.

Book Mobile

1. Write the title of the book and the names of the author and illustrator on the long strip.

2. Glue the long strip to a 4" x 12" (10 x 30.5 cm) strip of construction paper.

3. In each circle, draw a picture of a character. Write the character's name.

4. On the back of the circle, write a sentence describing the character.

5. Cut out the pieces.

6. Form a ring with the long strip and tape the ends together.

7. Cut three pieces of yarn, each about 6" (15 cm) long.

8. Using tape, attach the pieces of yarn to the back of the long strip. Tape a circle to the end of each piece of yarn.

9. Cut three 20" (51 cm) pieces of yarn. Tape one piece of yarn to each hole on the top edge of the mobile. Tie the pieces together at the top and hang.

A Book Mobile
Individual Book Report Project

1. Write the information on the pattern pieces.
2. Draw each character. Color, cut out, and make the mobile.

character's name

character's name

character's name

A Book Mobile

Illustrator:

Title:

Author:

My Name:

The Setting Pop-up

Individual Book Report Project

Literature Skill Focus: Identifying the story setting

1. Teaching the Literature Skill

- Review the elements of the *setting*. Remind students that the setting is *where* and *when* the story takes place.

- Read *The Tale of Peter Rabbit* by Beatrix Potter to your class. Help students identify the "when" part of the setting (a summer day). Clues that lead to this conclusion include: Farmer MacGregor working in the garden, vegetables growing, hot sun, Mother Rabbit out picking berries.

- Ask students to recall some clues to the place where the story was set. They might say, "under the root of the fir tree" or "in the garden." Help students reach the conclusion that the story took place in a garden near the woods.

2. Modeling the Project

- Demonstrate how to make the setting pop-up for *The Tale of Peter Rabbit*.

3. Reading at Home

- Have students choose a fiction book from the library. They take home the book and their copy of the pop-up pattern on page 51.

- After reading the book, the student works with the parent to make the setting pop-up. The student returns the book and the pop-up to school.

4. Sharing the Book Projects

- When the projects have been returned, display them, have a class discussion about the literature skill in students' books, or have partners share their projects.

Setting Pop-up

1. Write the title of the book and the names of the author and illustrator on the pattern.

2. Write information about the setting on the two small rectangles. One is for time and the other is for place. Be sure to support the information with clues from the book.

3. Cut out the rectangles and the pop-up pattern.

4. Fold and cut the pop-up form.

5. Glue the *Time* and *Place* rectangles to the pop-up tabs.

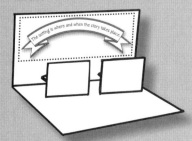

The setting is where and when the story takes place.

50

The Setting Pop-up
Individual Book Report Project

1. Write information on the patterns.
2. Make the pop-up tabs.
3. Glue the *Time* and *Place* pieces to the tabs.

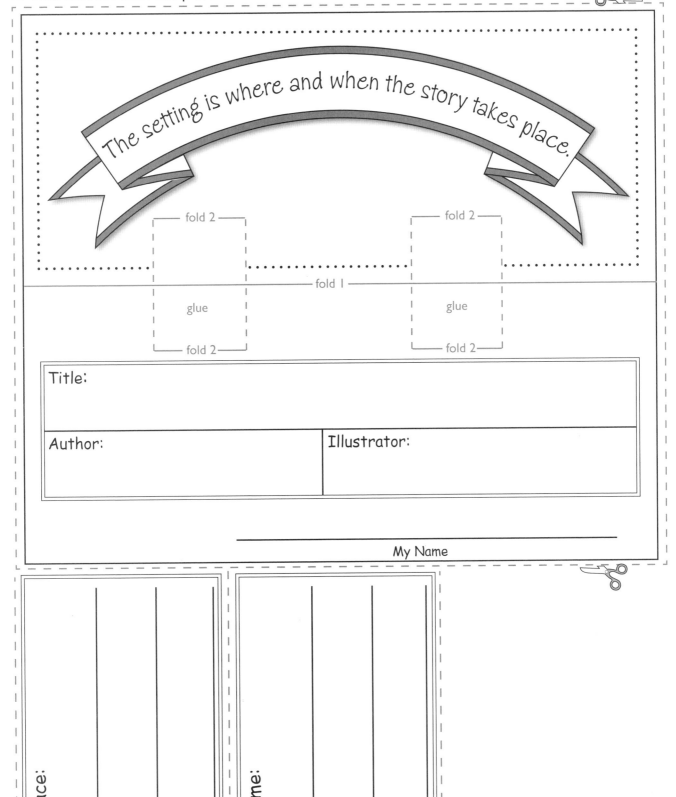

The setting is where and when the story takes place.

fold 2   fold 2

fold 1

glue   glue

fold 2   fold 2

Title:

Author: Illustrator:

My Name

Place:

Time:

A Pocket Diary

Individual Book Report Project

Literature Skill Focus: Writing about the life of a story character

1. Teaching the Literature Skill

- Read a portion of one of Peggy Parish's Amelia Bedelia books to your students.

- Have them describe Amelia Bedelia and recall what she did in the excerpt you read. Ask students to imagine how Amelia Bedelia might write about what she did in a diary.

- Model writing a simple diary entry about an event from the excerpt. Use one to three short sentences.

2. Modeling the Project

- Demonstrate how to make a pocket diary for the Amelia Bedelia book you read. Use the entry you modeled for the class.

3. Reading at Home

- Have students choose a fiction book from the library. They take home the book and their copy of the pocket diary pattern on page 53.

- After reading the book, the student and parent create a diary that might have been written by the main character. The student returns the book and the pocket diary to school.

4. Sharing the Book Projects

- When the projects have been returned, display them, have a class discussion about the literature skill in students' books, or have partners share their projects.

Pocket Diary

1. Cut out the pocket diary forms. Fill in the information on the cover, including the name of the character who is writing the diary.

2. At the top, staple the three diary pages to the cover of the diary.

3. Write three short entries inside the diary. Write about something that happened in the story.

4. Write your name on the back.

☆ Pocket Diary
Book Report ☆

Amelia Bedelia
Character

Amelia Bedelia Helps Out
Title

Peggy Parish
Author

A Pocket Diary
Individual Book Report Project

Fill out the information on the cover. Cut out the pockets. Write 3 diary entries on the pages.
Staple the cover and the pages together. Write your name on the back of the diary.

☆ Pocket Diary ☆
Book Report

_____
Character

_____
Title

_____
Author

Date: _____

Date: _____

Date: _____

A Book Report Box

Individual Book Report Project

Literature Skill Focus: Recalling story elements

1. Teaching the Literature Skill

- Read *How I Became a Pirate* by Melinda Long with your students. Jeremy Jacob is building a sand castle when a pirate band invites him to join them in burying their treasure. His adventures lead him to appreciate the comforts of home.

- Discuss how the setting, the characters, and the events combine to tell the story. Have students identify the setting and the characters. Then ask students to name one important event in the story. Have them explain why they think that event is an important one. Different students will choose different events.

2. Modeling the Project

- Demonstrate how to make a book report box for *How I Became a Pirate.*

3. Reading at Home

- Have students choose a fiction book from the library. They take home the book and their copy of the stand-up pattern on page 55.

- After reading the book, the student works with the parent to list story elements and make the book report box. The student returns the book and the book report box to school.

4. Sharing the Book Projects

- When the projects have been returned, display them, have a class discussion about the literature skill in students' books, or have partners share their projects.

Book Report Box

1. Write the information on each side of the box pattern.

2. Cut out the box and fold along the fold lines. Glue or tape where indicated.

3. On 3" x 3" (7.5 cm) squares of paper, write important events from the story. Tell why those events are important.

4. Place the papers inside the box.

A Book Report Box
Individual Book Report Project

Fill in the information. Fold where shown. Cut on the lines. Tape or glue to make a box.
On 3" x 3" (7.5 cm) squares of paper, write important events from the story. Tell why the events are important.

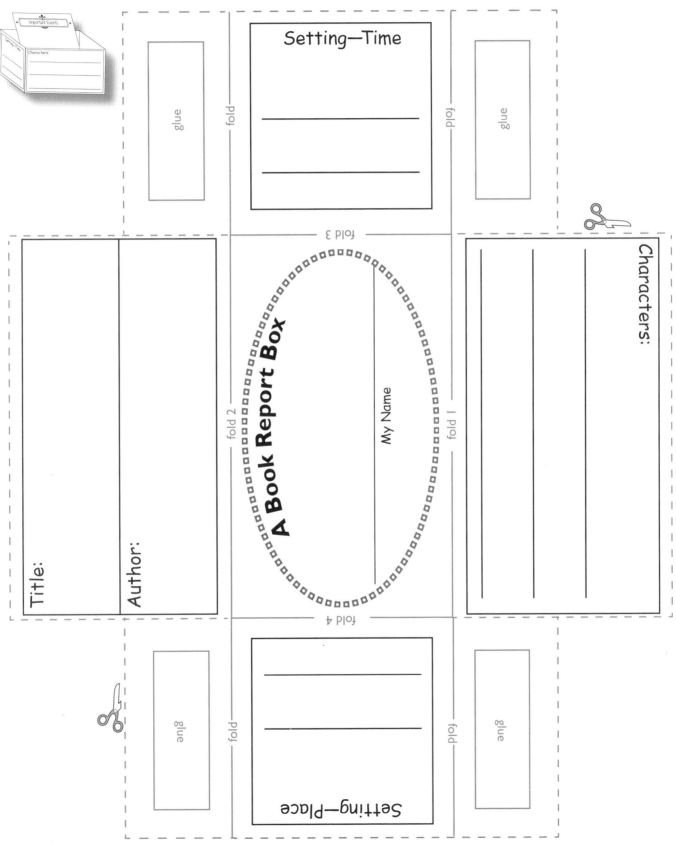

A Character Trading Card

Individual Book Report Project

Literature Skill Focus: Recalling facts about a character

1. Teaching the Literature Skill

- Briefly review the term *character* with your class. Explain that authors give clues in stories that help the reader learn about the characters.

- Read *Supergrandpa* by David M. Schwartz to your class. This book is based on a true story from Sweden. Gustaf Hakansson, age 66, is excluded from a 1,000-mile bicycle race because of his age. Determined to participate, he cycles 600 miles to the finish line.

- Ask the students to listen closely to learn all they can about Gustaf. When you have finished the story, help students recall Grandpa's name, age, hair color, eye color, and hobbies. Using student input, write a sentence that summarizes something important that Gustaf did.

2. Modeling the Project

- Model how to make the trading card for *Supergrandpa*.

3. Reading at Home

- Have students choose a fiction book from the library. They take home the book and their copy of the trading card pattern on page 57.

- After reading the book, the student works with the parent to fill in the information and complete the trading card. The student returns the book and the trading card to school.

4. Sharing the Book Projects

- When the projects have been returned, display them, have a class discussion about the literature skill in students' books, or have partners share their projects.

Trading Card

1. Write the character's name on the card. Fill in the rest of the information.

2. Write one sentence about something important the character did.

3. Draw a picture of the character.

4. Cut out the card and fold it along the fold line.

5. Glue the two sides together.

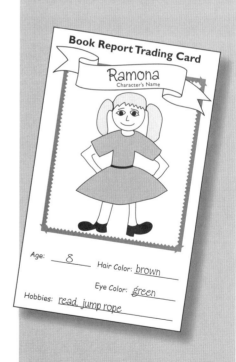

Book Report Trading Card

Ramona
Character's Name

Age: 8   Hair Color: brown

Eye Color: green

Hobbies: read, jump rope

A Character Trading Card
Individual Book Report Project

1. Write information about the character on the card.
2. Draw the character's picture.
3. Cut out, fold, and glue the card.

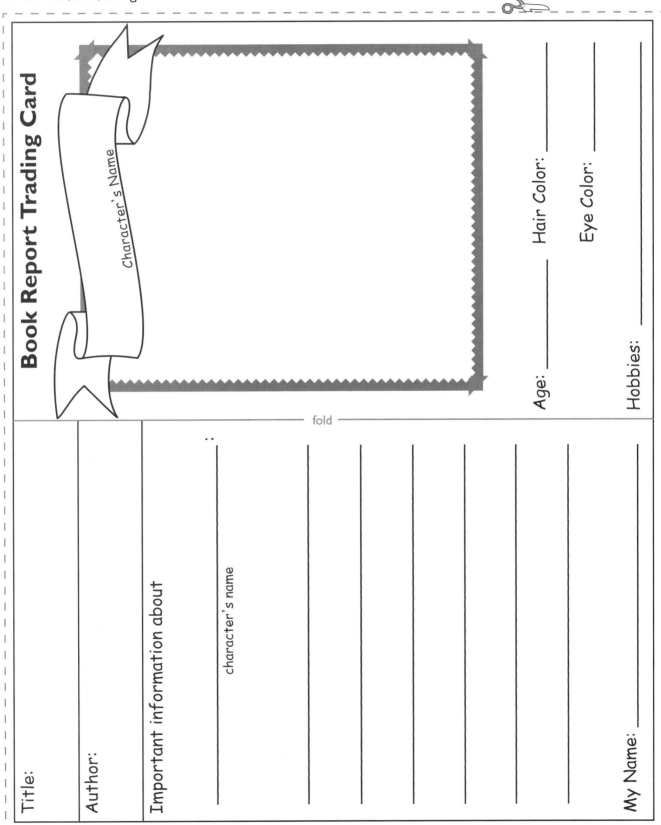

Book Report Trading Card

Character's Name

Age: _____

Hair Color: _____

Eye Color: _____

Hobbies: _____

fold

Title: _____

Author: _____

Important information about _____

character's name

_____
_____
_____
_____
_____
_____
_____
_____

My Name: _____

A Paper Bag Puppet

Individual Book Report Project

Literature Skill Focus: Retelling a story from a character's point of view

1. Teaching the Literature Skill

- Introduce or review the term *point of view*. The point of view is the angle from which the author tells the story. The story may be told by one of the characters or by someone outside the story.

- Tell students that a character's point of view might change the character's perception of an event. Ask students to briefly retell the story of the three little pigs. Explain that the story is traditionally told from the pigs' point of view. We know this because each pig tells his own story.

- Read *The True Story of the 3 Little Pigs* by Jon Scieszka to your class. Explain that this telling is from the wolf's point of view. Discuss some of the differences in the two versions of the same story.

2. Modeling the Project

- Demonstrate how to make a paper bag puppet for the wolf.

3. Reading at Home

- Have students choose a fiction book from the library. They take home the book and their copy of the puppet pattern on page 59.

- After reading the book, the student works with the parent to make a paper bag puppet. The student returns the book and the puppet to school.

4. Sharing the Book Projects

- When the projects have been returned, make time to have the "puppets" retell stories from their point of view. You may also want to display the puppets or have partners share their projects.

Paper Bag Puppet

1. Fill in the information about the book and the character on the form on page 59.

2. Cut out and glue the information to the paper bag.

3. Decide which character is going to retell the story. Draw a picture of that character in the circle.

4. Cut out the circle and glue it to the bottom of the paper bag.

5. Practice retelling the story using the puppet.

A Paper Bag Puppet
Book Report
Glue this to the back of the paper bag.

Title: The True Story of the 3 Little Pigs
Author: Jon Scieszka   Illustrator: Lane Smith
Who tells the story? the wolf
My Name: Jose

A Paper Bag Puppet
Individual Book Report Project

1. Fill in the label and glue it to the bag.

2. In the circle, draw a picture of the character who is going to tell the story.

3. Cut out the circle and glue it to the bag.

A Paper Bag Puppet
Book Report

Glue this to the front of the paper bag.

Title:	
Author:	Illustrator:
Who tells the story?	
My Name:	

The Big-Mouth Hippo

Individual Book Report Project

Literature Skill Focus: Recommending a book to peers

1. Teaching the Literature Skill

- Ask students how they choose books from the library. Explain that today's skill is making a good recommendation. Tell students that good recommendations give specific information about the book.

- Read *A Pocket Full of Kisses* by Audrey Penn to your class. Model how to make a recommendation specific to that book.

   Specific: I liked *A Pocket Full of Kisses* because Mother Raccoon listened to Chester's problem and didn't put him down. She let him know that he was important and that the baby was important, too. I recommend this book to kids who have new baby sisters or brothers.

   Nonspecific: *A Pocket Full of Kisses* was a nice story. It had pretty pictures.

2. Modeling the Project

- Demonstrate how to make a big-mouth hippo for *A Pocket Full of Kisses.* Use the recommendations from the class discussions.

3. Reading at Home

- Have students choose a book from the library. They take home the book and their copy of the hippo pattern on page 61.

- After reading the book, the student and parent write a recommendation for it in the hippo's mouth. The student returns the book and the hippo to school.

4. Sharing the Book Projects

- When the projects have been returned, display them, have a class discussion about the literature skill in students' books, or have partners share their projects.

Big-Mouth Hippo

1. Write your recommendation on the lines inside the hippo's mouth.

2. On the next mouth-shaped piece of the pattern, fill in the title of the book and the names of the author and illustrator.

3. Color and cut out the top of the hippo's mouth.

4. Glue the two mouth pieces in place.

5. Finish coloring your hippo.

6. Glue it to a 6" x 8½" (15 x 21.5 cm) piece of construction paper.

A Great Book

The Big-Mouth Hippo
Individual Book Report Project

1. Fill in the forms.
2. Color and cut out the pieces.
3. Glue the pieces in place.

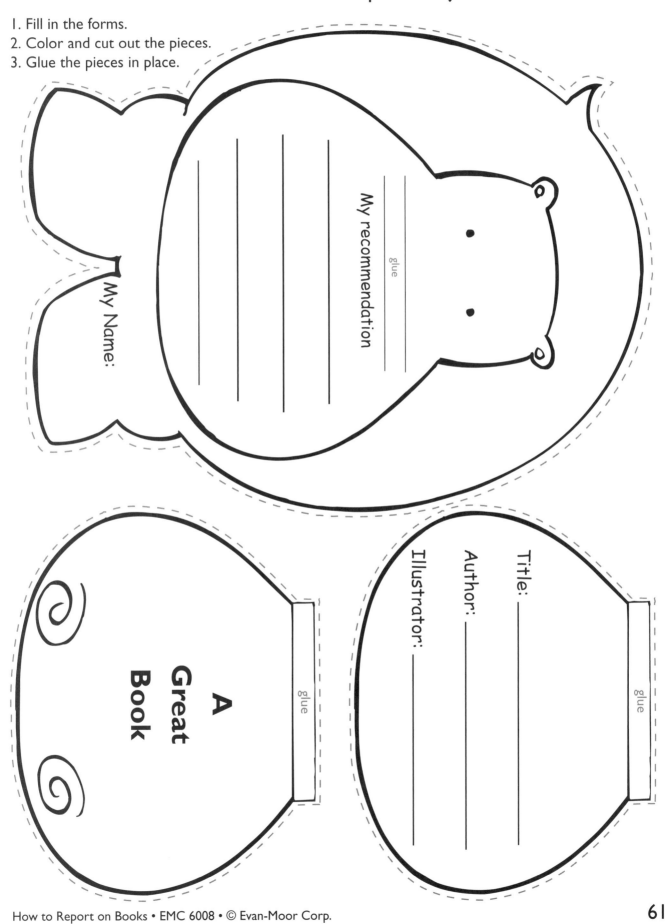

My Name:

My recommendation

glue

Title:

Author:

Illustrator:

glue

A
Great
Book

glue

A Riddle Pop-up
Individual Book Report Project

Literature Skill Focus: Describing a character

1. Teaching the Literature Skill

- Tell students they are going to write a riddle for their book report.

- Read *Thumbelina* by Hans Christian Andersen to the class. Work together to compose three clues about Thumbelina. Think aloud about what makes a good clue as you are working. For example, the clue has to describe Thumbelina and tell something about her. A model riddle might be:

  > *Tiny as your thumb,*
  > *Born from a tulip,*
  > *Everyone loves her.*

2. Modeling the Project

- Using the clues for *Thumbelina,* model how to make the project.

3. Reading at Home

- Have students choose a fiction book from the library. They take home the book and their copy of the pop-up pattern on page 63.

- After reading the book, the student works with the parent to write a riddle about a character in the book and to make the riddle pop-up. The student returns the book and the pop-up to school.

4. Sharing the Book Projects

- When the projects have been returned, display them, have a class discussion about the literature skill in students' books, or have partners share their projects.

Riddle Pop-up

1. Fill in the book title, author, illustrator, and your name on the form on page 63.

2. Cut out the pattern. Fold on the fold lines.

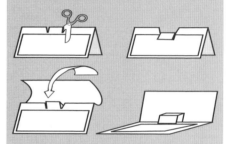

3. Glue the pop-up inside a 7" x 8" (18 x 20 cm) piece of construction paper folded in half.

4. Draw the character. Glue the picture to the tab.

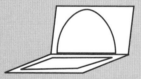

5. Glue the clues to the outside of the folder.

6. Read your riddle. Look inside for the answer.

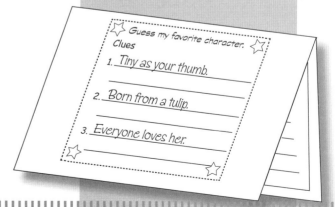

A Riddle Pop-up
Individual Book Report Project

Fill out the information. Cut out and fold the pattern. Glue it inside a 7" x 8" (18 x 20 cm) piece of construction paper folded in half. Write clues and glue them on the outside. Draw and label the character. Glue the picture on the pop-up tab.

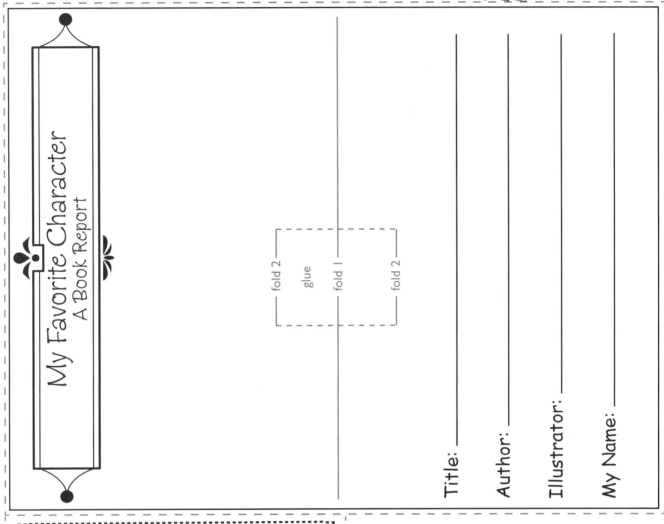

My Favorite Character
A Book Report

fold 2

glue

fold 1

fold 2

Title:

Author:

Illustrator:

My Name:

Guess my favorite character.

Clues

1. _____

_____

2. _____

_____

3. _____

_____

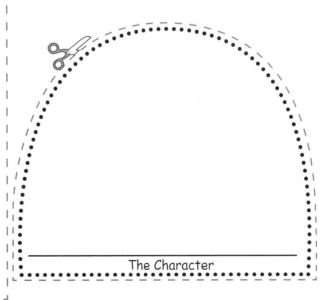

The Character

A Monkey Bookmark

Individual Book Report Project

Literature Skill Focus: Summarizing a story

1. Teaching the Literature Skill
- Explain to students that you will be asking them to summarize the book you are about to read. This is a difficult skill for students to grasp. Introduce the word *summary* by saying it is like a sum in an addition problem. A summary adds up the important things that happened in a story. Describe what a good summary might include. It might include the main character, the location, the problem, and the solution.

- Read *The Little House* by Virginia Lee Burton to your class. Help students develop a short summary of the story, for example, a busy city grows up around an empty little house. The house is moved to a new location in the country, where a new family loves it.

2. Modeling the Project
- Demonstrate how to make a monkey bookmark for *The Little House*. Use the summary from the lesson.

3. Reading at Home
- Have students choose a book from the library. They take home the book and their copy of the bookmark pattern on page 65.

- After reading the book, the student works with the parent to write a book summary and make the bookmark. The student returns the book and the bookmark to school.

4. Sharing the Book Projects
- When the projects have been returned, display them, have a class discussion about the literature skill in students' books, or have partners share their projects.

Monkey Bookmark

1. Fill in the information on the form on page 65.
2. Color the monkey and cut it out.
3. Use a fastener to attach the tail.
4. Use your bookmark to mark your place in the next book you read.

A Book Report

Author: Virginia Lee Burton

Summary:
A busy city grows up around an empty little house. The house is moved to a new location in the country, where a new family loves it.

Title: The Little House

My Name: Zoe

A Monkey Bookmark
Individual Book Report Project

1. Fill in the information.
2. Color the monkey and cut it out.
3. Attach the tail to the monkey.

Title:

My Name:

A Book Report

Author:

Summary:

Ssssso Many Facts

Individual Book Report Project

Literature Skill Focus: Recalling facts

1. Teaching the Literature Skill

- Remind students that even though they read a make-believe story, they can learn true information.

- Read *Pinduli* by Janell Cannon to the class. Pinduli is a little hyena who comes across a pack of wild dogs. The pack makes fun of Pinduli. Ask students to listen for facts about hyenas.

- Have students tell the information they have learned. Write each fact on a chart. Check the facts with the text. An informational article is included at the end of the book.

2. Modeling the Project

- Demonstrate how to make a fact snake for *Pinduli*. On each section of the snake, write a fact from the chart.

3. Reading at Home

- Have students choose a fiction book from the library. They take home the book and their copy of the fact snake pattern on page 67.

- After reading the book, the student works with the parent to recall facts they have learned from the book and to make the project. The student returns the book and the project to school.

4. Sharing the Book Projects

- When the projects have been returned, display them, have a class discussion about the literature skill in students' books, or have partners share their projects.

Fact Snake

1. Fill in the title of the book and the names of the author and illustrator on the form on page 67.

2. Write a fact on each section of the snake.

3. Color the snake.

4. Cut out the snake and lift it by the head to see the spiral.

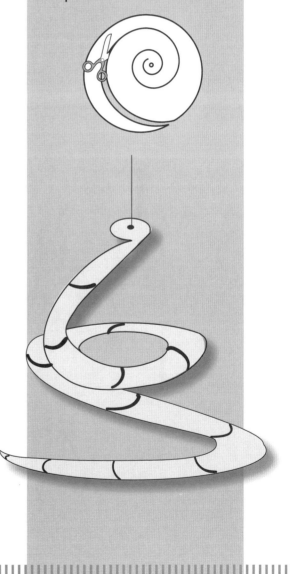

Sssso Many Facts

Individual Book Report Project

1. Fill in the information.
2. Write a fact on each section of the snake.
3. Color the snake and cut it out.

A Book Report

Title:

Author:

Fact 3:

My Name:

Fact 2:

Illustrator:

Fact 4:

Fact 1:

Accordion Book

Individual Book Report Project

Literature Skill Focus: Identifying the problem and solution

1. Teaching the Literature Skill

- Briefly explain to students that the events in some stories present a *problem* and then the *solution*. There is often one main problem and many smaller problems.

- Read *The Mysterious Tadpole* by Steven Kellogg. Ask students to identify some of the problems in the book. For example, Louis doesn't have money to buy Alphonse's cheeseburgers, and Alphonse outgrows the bathtub and every other place in the house.

- Have students choose a main problem. This might be that Alphonse can't stay in the school swimming pool. Then ask them to tell how the main problem was solved. For example, the librarian solved the problem. She used Alphonse to hunt for sunken treasure. The bounty provided money to build Alphonse's own swimming pool.

2. Modeling the Project

- Demonstrate how to make a folded accordion book for *The Mysterious Tadpole*.

3. Reading at Home

- Students choose a fiction book from the library. They take home the book, their copy of the book panel patterns on page 69, and a 6" x 18" (15 x 45.5 cm) strip of construction paper.

- After reading the book, the student and parent make a folded book describing the problem and solution. The student returns the library book and the accordion book to school.

4. Sharing the Book Projects

- When the projects have been returned, display them, have a class discussion about the literature skill in students' books, or have partners share their projects.

Folded Accordion Book

1. Accordion fold a 6" x 18" (15 x 45.5 cm) strip of construction paper as shown.

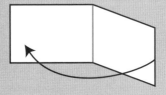

2. Fill in the information on the book panels on page 69.

3. Cut out the panels and glue them onto the accordion book.

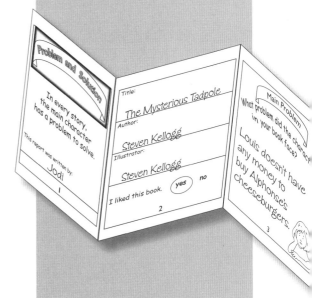

Accordion Book
Individual Book Report Project

1. Make an accordion book with a 6" x 18" (15 x 45.5 cm) strip of paper.
2. Draw a picture of the problem and the solution.
3. Glue the panels onto the book.

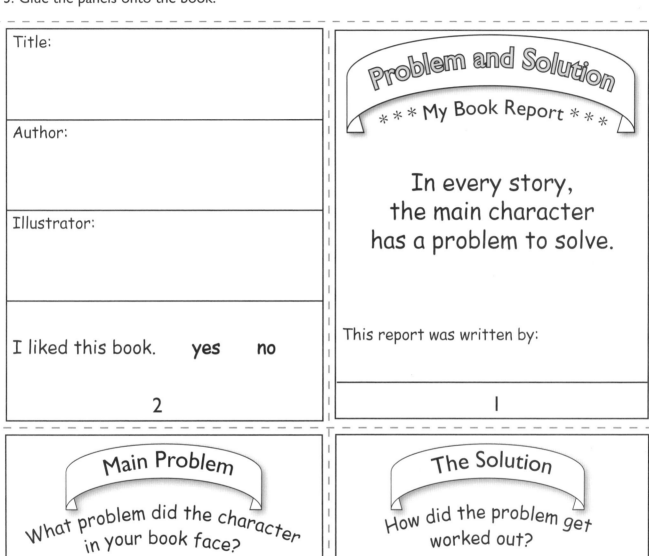

Title:

Author:

Illustrator:

I liked this book.   yes   no

2

Problem and Solution

*** My Book Report ***

In every story,
the main character
has a problem to solve.

This report was written by:

_____

1

Main Problem

What problem did the character
in your book face?

3

The Solution

How did the problem get
worked out?

4

My Book Movie

Individual Book Report Project

Literature Skill Focus: Retelling the story

1. Teaching the Literature Skill

- Review briefly the idea of retelling a story. Remind students to retell what happened first, next, and last.

- Read *The Name Jar* by Yangsook Choi to your class. Help students choose the main events in the story. List them on a chart. The main events are: Unhei has just come from Korea. The kids on the bus tease her about her name. She tells her class she hasn't decided on a new name. The kids put names in a jar and put the jar on her desk. Unhei keeps her Korean name after all.

2. Modeling the Project

- Reproduce the movie screen pattern on page 71. Demonstrate how to make a pull-through movie for *The Name Jar.*

3. Reading at Home

- Have students choose a fiction book from the library. They take home the book and their copy of the pattern on page 71.

- After reading the book, the student and parent make a pull-through movie to retell the story. The student returns the book and the pull-through movie to school.

4. Sharing the Book Projects

- When the projects have been returned, display them, have a class discussion about the literature skill in students' books, or have partners share their projects.

Pull-through Movie

1. Write the title of the book and the names of the author and illustrator on the form.

2. In the appropriate boxes, draw pictures representing what happened first, next, and last in the book you read.

3. Cut out the movie strip.

4. On the form, cut two slits where indicated.

5. Insert the movie strip in the movie screen.

6. Then pull it through slowly and watch your movie.

How to Report on Books • EMC 6008 • © Evan-Moor Corp.

My Book Movie
Individual Book Report Project

1. Fill in the book information.
2. Draw pictures of what happened first, next, and last.
3. Cut out the movie strip.
4. Insert the movie strip in the screen and pull through.

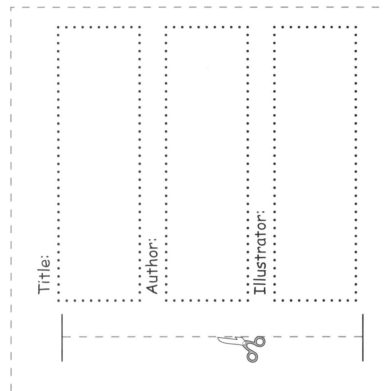

Title:

Author:

Illustrator:

My Name:

Pull movie strip through here.

My Book Movie

Let me show you about the book!

last

next

first

pull movie strip

A Fan

Individual Book Report Project

Literature Skill Focus: Identifying book information

1. Teaching the Literature Skill

- Review with your students the information that is found on the book jacket and the inside pages. This information includes the title, author, illustrator, publisher, year the book was written, and dedication.

- Look at the book *Old Black Fly* by Jim Aylesworth. Help students locate each piece of information you have just discussed. Then read the book.

2. Modeling the Project

- Show students how to make a fan for *Old Black Fly*.

3. Reading at Home

- Have students choose a book from the library. They take home the book and their copy of the fan pattern on page 73.

- After reading the book, the student and parent make a fan. Together, they record information about the book on the fan. The student returns the book and the fan to school.

4. Sharing the Book Projects

- When the projects have been returned, display them, have a class discussion about the literature skill in students' books, or have partners share their projects.

Fan

1. Fill in the information in each section of the fan.

2. Color the fan in bright colors.

3. Cut out the fan and fold it.

4. Use a paper clip to secure the bottom.

A Fan
Individual Book Report Project

Fill in the information about the book. Color the form, cut it out, and fold it into a fan. ✄

I'm a FAN of this book.

Great Book!

Signed: _____

Dedication:

fold

Publisher:

fold

Illustrator:

fold

Author:

fold

Title:

A Book Visor

Individual Book Report Project

Literature Skill Focus: Evaluating a book

1. Teaching the Literature Skill

- List four or five of your students' favorite books on a chart. Under each book title, list one thing the students really enjoyed. For example, the pictures were funny, the story made me laugh, it was about a favorite animal, the story made me feel good inside. Ask your students to tell you what makes a good book. Using their ideas, develop a list of criteria to evaluate a book they are reading.

- Read *Town Mouse Country Mouse* by Jan Brett. Have students evaluate the book using the list. Model how to write a sentence using the list. For example, *Town Mouse Country Mouse* is a great book because it has an interesting story. The story makes me laugh. The peepholes are fun because you get to peek ahead to see what is going to happen.

2. Modeling the Project

- Demonstrate how to make a book visor for *Town Mouse Country Mouse*. Write the model evaluation sentence about the book.

3. Reading at Home

- Have students choose a book from the library. They take home the book and their copy of the visor pattern on page 75.

- After reading the book, the student and parent fill in the information on the visor pattern. The student returns the book and the pattern to school. Complete the visors as part of a classroom center.

4. Sharing the Book Projects

- When the projects have been returned, display them, have a class discussion about the literature skill in students' books, or have partners share their projects.

Book Visor

1. Write a sentence on the form on page 75 telling why you liked the book.

2. Draw a character from the book in the circle. Write the book's title and the names of the author and illustrator.

3. Cut out the visor pattern.

4. Glue the cutout to a recycled file folder or other sturdy paper. Trim around the edges.

5. Punch holes. Attach yarn or string to complete the visor.

Title: Harry the Dirty Dog

Author: Gene Zion

Illustrator: Margaret Bloy Graham

The Character

My Name: Sammy

I liked this book because I like dogs that play in the dirt.

A Good Book Visor

A Book Visor
Individual Book Report Project

1. Draw a picture in the circle.
2. Cut out the visor. Glue it to a file folder.
3. Trim around the edges.
4. Punch holes. Attach yarn ties.

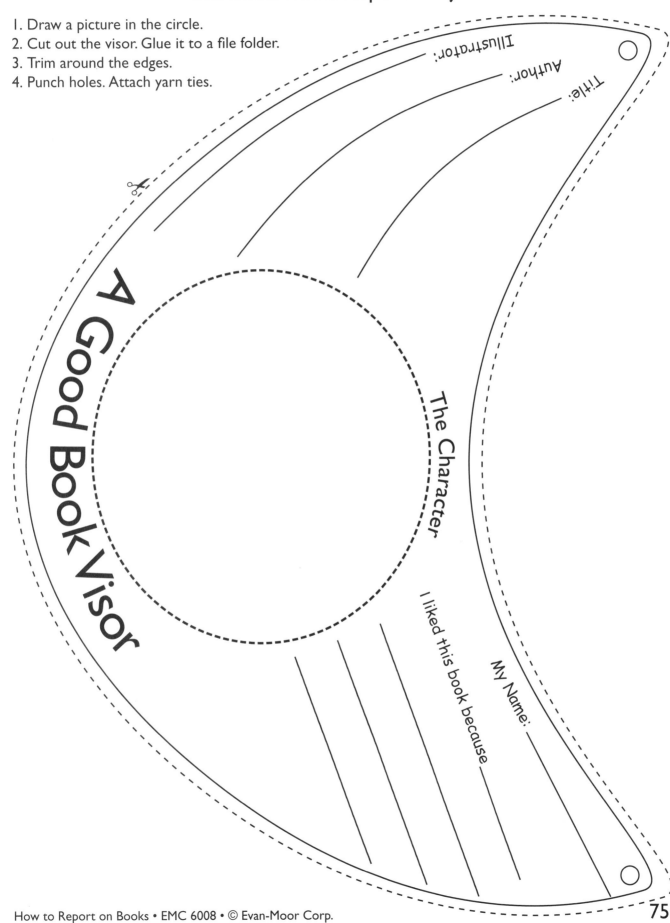

A Good Book Visor

Title:
Author:
Illustrator:

The Character

My Name: _____

I liked this book because _____

A Character T-Shirt

Individual Book Report Project

Literature Skill Focus: Predicting a character's actions

1. Teaching the Literature Skill

- Explain to students that if the author does a good job of making the story character real, the reader will be able to predict what the character would like and how the character would act in new situations. Discuss how we know about a character's likes and dislikes.

- Read *Anansi and the Talking Melon* by Eric A. Kimmel. Have students tell you what they know about Anansi. For example, Anansi loves to eat melons. Anansi is lazy. Anansi likes to play tricks.

- Have students speculate about the kinds of things Anansi might do in the future. You might ask, "What would Anansi do if he saw a whale growing giant strawberries?"

2. Modeling the Project

- Demonstrate how to make a T-shirt for Anansi.

3. Reading at Home

- Have students choose a fiction book from the library. They take home the book and their copy of the T-shirt pattern on page 77.

- After reading the book, the student and parent create a T-shirt for the main character of the book. The student returns the book and the T-shirt to school.

4. Sharing the Book Projects

- When the projects have been returned, display them, have a class discussion about the literature skill in students' books, or have partners share their projects.

T-Shirt

1. Write the title of the book and the names of the author and illustrator on the bottom of the form on page 77.

2. Across the middle of the shirt, write the character's name in letters and colors the character would like.

3. Color the T-shirt a color that the character would like. Add patterns and pictures that would be appropriate for the character.

4. Cut out the T-shirt pattern.

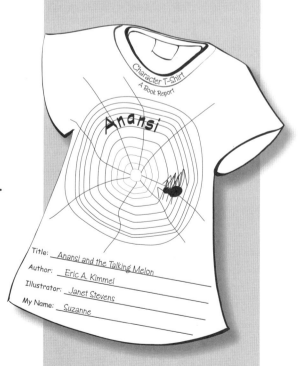

Title: *Anansi and the Talking Melon*
Author: *Eric A. Kimmel*
Illustrator: *Janet Stevens*
My Name: *Suzanne*

A Character T-Shirt
Individual Book Report Project

1. Design a T-shirt for the main character in the book you just read.
2. Write the character's name across the middle.

Character T-Shirt
A Book Report

Title: _____

Author: _____

Illustrator: _____

My Name: _____

Butterfly Word Catcher

Individual Book Report Project

Literature Skill Focus: Selecting words and phrases to remember

1. Teaching the Literature Skill

- Using well-written picture books as a model for excellent descriptive language is important.

- Read *Owl Moon* by Jane Yolen to your class. Have students listen for words or phrases that "fly" off the page. The words should stand out and make a special picture in the reader's mind.

- Record some of the picture language on a chart. For example: The trees stood as still as giant statues. My nose and cheeks felt cold and hot at the same time. The snow was whiter than the milk in a cereal bowl.

2. Modeling the Project

- Demonstrate how to make the butterfly word catcher. Use the picture language from *Owl Moon*.

3. Reading at Home

- Have students choose a well-written picture book from the library. The students take home the book and a copy of the pattern on page 79.

- After reading the book, the student and parent make the butterfly. They record words and phrases that "flew off the page" on the butterfly's spots. The student returns the book and the butterfly to school.

4. Sharing the Book Projects

- When the projects have been returned, add the tissue paper strips and display the butterflies, have a class discussion about the literature skill in students' books, or have partners share their projects.

Butterfly Word Catcher

1. Write the title of the book and the names of the author and illustrator on the pattern.

2. Pick out four words or phrases that you want to remember.

3. Write them on each of the butterfly's spots. Outline each one with color.

4. Color the butterfly. Cut it out and glue it onto a sheet of construction paper.

5. Trim the edges of the mounted butterfly, leaving a colorful border.

6. Glue tissue paper streamers to the butterfly's body.

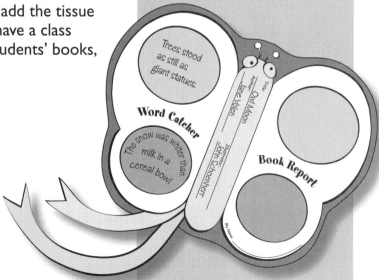

How to Report on Books • EMC 6008 • © Evan-Moor Corp.

A Butterfly Word Catcher
Individual Book Report Project

1. Pick out four words or phrases from your book and write one on each spot.
2. Color and cut out the butterfly.
3. Glue it onto a sheet of construction paper. Trim the edges, leaving a border.

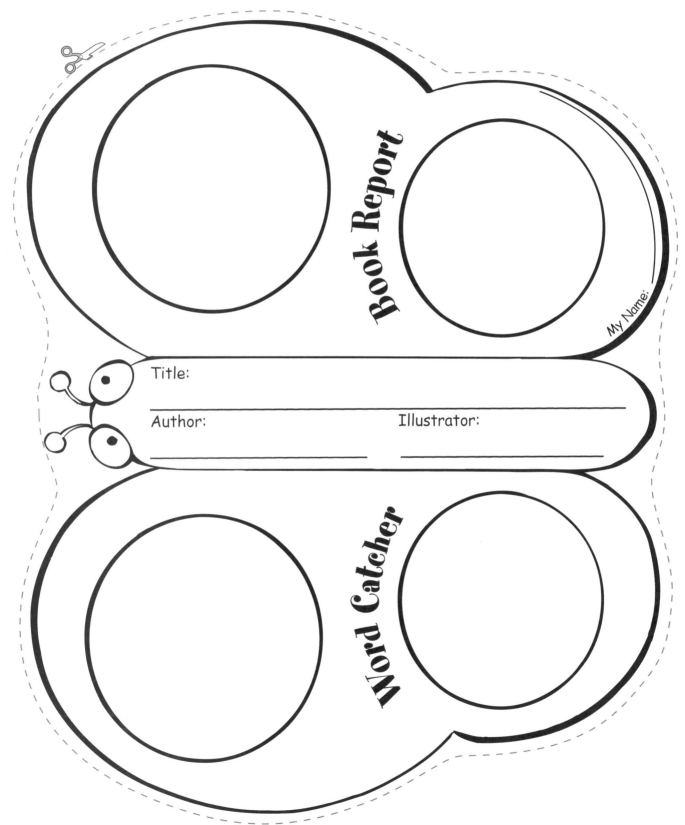

Book Report

My Name:

Title:

Author: Illustrator:

Word Catcher

Parent Letter
Support Independent Reading

Dear Parents,

The project described on the attached sheet is to be completed when your child has finished reading his or her independent reading book. Please support your child's independent reading. Ask your child to tell you all about the book. Retelling and summarizing stories are important comprehension skills. Then help your child complete the project as needed. Initial your child's Reading Record.

Thank you for encouraging your child's love of reading.

Sincerely,

Dear Parents,

The project described on the attached sheet is to be completed when your child has finished reading his or her independent reading book. Please support your child's independent reading. Ask your child to tell you all about the book. Retelling and summarizing stories are important comprehension skills. Then help your child complete the project as needed. Initial your child's Reading Record.

Thank you for encouraging your child's love of reading.

Sincerely,

Group
Book Report
Projects

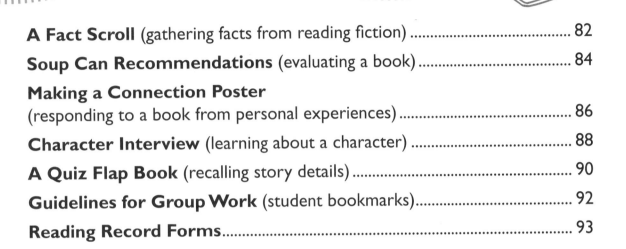

A Fact Scroll

Group Book Report Project

Literature Skill Focus: Gathering facts from reading fiction

1. Giving the Assignment

- Briefly review the difference between real and make-believe stories (nonfiction and fiction). Explain to students that sometimes a fictional story is based on real events or presents real information. If it is appropriate for your students, introduce the term *realistic fiction*.

- Explain to students that in their small groups they will be reading and finding factual information. Each group will create a scroll that presents some of the facts the group has discovered.

2. Reading with a Small Group

- Assign students to work in small groups. Provide multiple copies of several fiction books that include factual information. Assign a book to each group.

- Each student reads the book independently and completes the note taker on page 83.

- In their groups, students discuss the factual information they learned by reading the book. Using their note takers, they create a master list of important facts they learned from the book. Group members create a fact scroll by recording and illustrating facts on separate squares of construction paper. The squares are then taped together to form the scroll.

3. Sharing the Group Projects

- Invite each group to share its scroll with the class. When all groups have reported, ask students if they believe the books presented facts in an interesting way.

Fact Scroll

1. On the note taker, write down five facts you learned.

2. For each group, cut seven 4" x 4" (10 cm) squares of construction paper and a 5" x 36" (13 x 91.5 cm) strip of butcher paper.

3. On the first square of construction paper, the group writes the title of the book, the name of the author, and the topic.

4. On the next five squares, group members write facts presented in the book and illustrate them. (Make additional squares as needed for large groups.)

5. The final square should be a list of the group members.

6. Glue the squares to the butcher paper scroll. Tape a tongue depressor or dowel to each side of the scroll. Roll the scroll. Tie it.

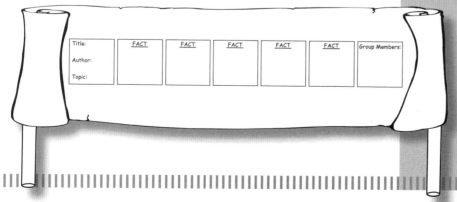

Note Taker for a Fact Scroll
Group Book Report Project

Title:

Author: Illustrator:

Facts I Learned

Sometimes a fictional story is based on real events
or presents true information.

1. _____

2. _____

3. _____

4. _____

5. _____

Completed by:

Soup Can Recommendations
Group Book Report Project

Literature Skill Focus: Evaluating a book

1. Giving the Assignment
- Briefly review the criteria you developed with your class for evaluating a book. If you haven't previously done so, discuss possible criteria. See page 60 for how to do this.

- Explain to students that they will be reading and discussing a book with their group members. Then they will each make an independent evaluation of the book.

2. Reading with a Small Group
- Assign students to work in small groups. Provide multiple copies of several books. Assign a book to each group. Each student should read the book independently.

- When students have finished reading, they discuss the book. Each group makes a label for their soup can.

- Each student writes a personal recommendation on a spoon pattern on page 85. The recommendation includes something about the book that the student liked. The student stores the recommendation in the soup can.

3. Sharing the Group Projects
- Display a copy of each book with the soup can full of recommendations in your classroom library area. Students looking for a book to read can review the recommendations before choosing a new book.

Soup Can Label

1. Measure the side of an empty soup can and cut construction paper to cover it.

2. Design the soup can label. Include book title, author, illustrator, and names of group members.

3. Glue the label around the can.

4. Each student writes an evaluation of the book on the spoon pattern on page 85 and folds it in half.

How to Report on Books • EMC 6008 • © Evan-Moor Corp.

Soup Can Recommendations
Group Book Report Project

1. Design a soup can label for your book.
2. Each group member writes an evaluation of the book on the spoon pattern.

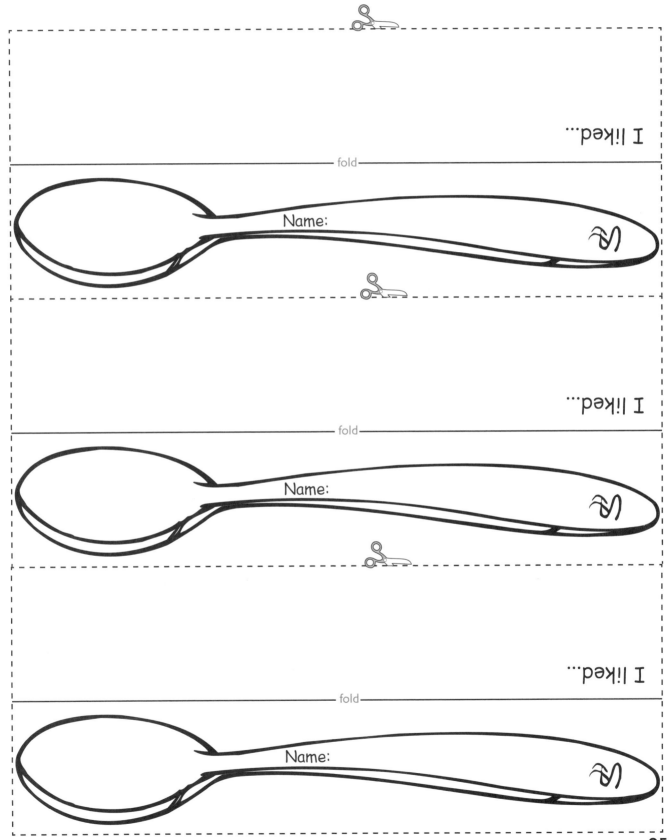

I liked....

fold

Name:

I liked....

fold

Name:

I liked....

fold

Name:

Making a Connection Poster

Group Book Report Project

Literature Skill Focus: Responding to a book from personal experiences

1. Giving the Assignment

- Ask students if they have ever had a special place for storing memories. Explain that the book you are about to read tells about a little girl who has a string with special buttons that represent her most precious memories.

- Read *The Memory String* by Eve Bunting to the class. Write the title and author across the top of a poster-size sheet of paper. Each student will write a statement about a personal connection to the book on a form (page 87) and glue it to the poster.

- Begin by modeling a sentence about a personal experience that connects to the book you read. For example, "I can understand why Laura loved her memory string. When you have something that belonged to somebody who died, it seems to be more than a memory because you can actually hold onto it." Invite other students to add their connections, as well.

2. Reading with a Small Group

- Assign students to work in small groups. Provide multiple copies of books for each group. Assign a book or let groups choose the book they will read.

- Each student reads the book independently. Students discuss the book. Then they create the poster.

- Group members write a personal connection on a copy of the form on page 87 and glue their connections to the poster.

3. Sharing the Group Projects

- Have each group post their group's connection poster in the classroom in a place where other students can add additional comments.

- Allow time for a brief introduction of each book. Copies of the books should be available for students from other groups.

Poster

1. Plan the poster to fit on a 12" x 18" (30.5 x 45.5 cm) sheet of construction paper. It should include the following:
   - the book's title and author
   - a brief summary
   - a border

2. On the forms (page 87), write individual comments about personal connections to the book.

3. Cut out the forms and glue them to the poster.

4. The group may add symbols from the story around the edges.

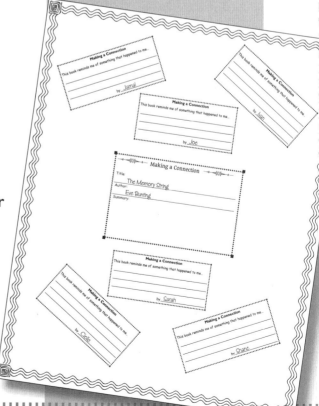

How to Report on Books • EMC 6008 • © Evan-Moor Corp.

Making a Connection Poster

Group Book Report Project

Making a Connection

Title:

Author:

Summary:

Making a Connection

This book reminds me of something that happened to me...

by _____

Making a Connection

This book reminds me of something that happened to me...

by _____

Making a Connection

This book reminds me of something that happened to me...

by _____

Character Interview

Group Book Report Project

Literature Skill Focus: Learning about a character

1. Giving the Assignment

- Discuss with the class the ways readers learn about characters. Sometimes the author tells us about a character. Sometimes other characters tell about a character. Sometimes the character's actions and thoughts tell readers about the character.

- Explain to students that they will be reading and discussing a book with their group members. They will learn about the main character and prepare an interview with that character to present to the class.

2. Reading with a Small Group

- Assign students to work in small groups. Provide multiple copies of books. Each group will read a different book. Students should read the book independently before the group activity.

- Students discuss the book. They decide which character is the main one. Beginning with the list of questions provided on page 89, group members discuss the character's answers. Once the group agrees on an answer, someone records it on the interview form.

- Finally, the group chooses one person to portray the main character and others to ask the questions. The group prepares a "television" interview to present to the class. If possible, videotape the interview for presentation.

3. Sharing the Group Projects

- Stage a "Meet the Character" day. Enjoy interviews prepared by each group.

- Have students think about which characters they would like to have as friends. Responses may be shared orally or written in a journal.

The Interview

1. As a group, choose the main character of the book.

2. Read the interview questions on page 89 and talk about how the character would answer the questions. Write down answers that would be appropriate.

3. Decide who will be the character and who will ask each question.

4. Practice the interview.

Character Interview

Group Book Report Project

Group Members:

Title:

Author: _____ Illustrator: _____

What is your name? _____

How old are you? _____

Where do you live? _____

_____

How would you describe your house? _____

_____

What is your favorite thing to do? _____

_____

What is your favorite color? _____

Do you have any pets? _____

What special problems do you have to solve? _____

_____

A Quiz Flap Book

Group Book Report Project

Literature Skill Focus: Recalling story details

1. Giving the Assignment

- Prepare several questions about a book that the class has read. Using *Anansi and the Talking Melon* by Eric Kimmel as an example, you might ask, "What kind of animal is Anansi?" or, "What did Anansi eat?" Write the questions and the answers on the flap pattern on page 91.

- Tell students that you are going to ask some questions to see if they remember specific events in the story. Ask the questions and confirm the answers by lifting the flap.

2. Reading with a Small Group

- Assign students to work in small groups. Provide multiple copies of books. Assign one book to each group. Each student should read the book independently.

- Students discuss the book. As a group, they write five questions and answers about the book on the flap patterns.

- Students create a cover for the quiz book. They bind the flaps together.

3. Sharing the Group Projects

- Display a copy of each book with its quiz flap book. Have students read the book and then "take the quiz" to see if they recall story details.

Quiz Flap Book

1. Provide the group with five quiz flap book forms on page 91. Fold the right side of the pattern inward to make the flap.

2. Write a question on the left side of the flap pattern.

3. Write the answer to the question in the answer box.

4. Cut a 4½" x 7½" (11.5 x 19 cm) piece of construction paper for the cover of the quiz book. On the cover, write the name of the book and the names of the author and illustrator. On the back of the cover, write the names of group members.

5. Use a piece of yarn or a metal ring to bind the flap pages and cover in a book.

A Quiz Flap Book

The Answer

A Quiz Flap Book
Group Book Report Project

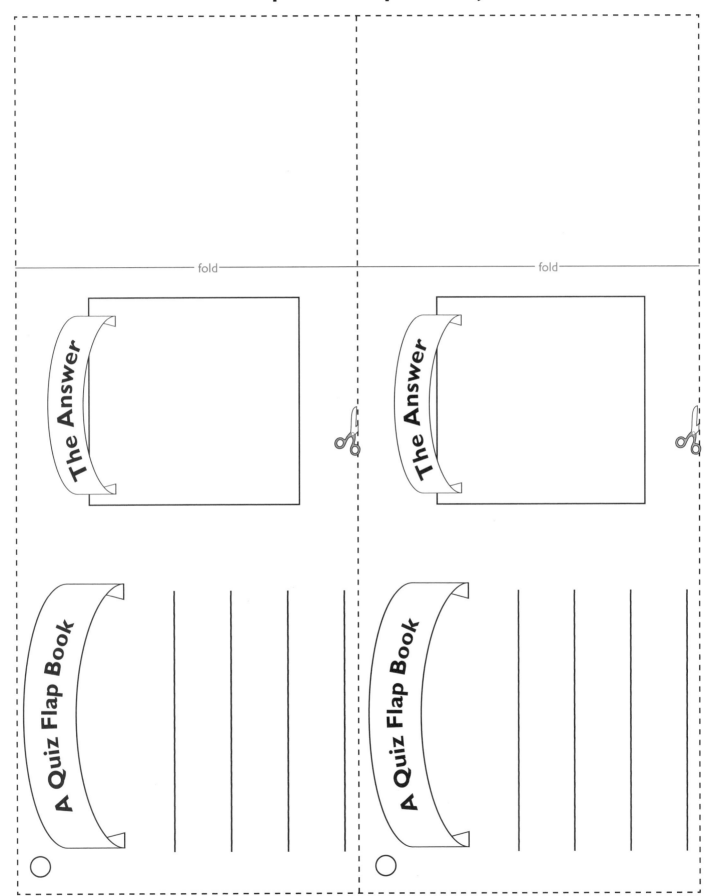

The Answer

A Quiz Flap Book

The Answer

A Quiz Flap Book

Guidelines for Group Work
Student Bookmarks

1. Respect other group members. Listen to everyone's ideas.
2. Make decisions only after everyone has had a chance to talk.
3. Stay on the topic. Follow the step-by-step directions.
4. Respect other class members. Use indoor voices.

1. Respect other group members. Listen to everyone's ideas.
2. Make decisions only after everyone has had a chance to talk.
3. Stay on the topic. Follow the step-by-step directions.
4. Respect other class members. Use indoor voices.

1. Respect other group members. Listen to everyone's ideas.
2. Make decisions only after everyone has had a chance to talk.
3. Stay on the topic. Follow the step-by-step directions.
4. Respect other class members. Use indoor voices.

1. Respect other group members. Listen to everyone's ideas.
2. Make decisions only after everyone has had a chance to talk.
3. Stay on the topic. Follow the step-by-step directions.
4. Respect other class members. Use indoor voices.

1. Respect other group members. Listen to everyone's ideas.
2. Make decisions only after everyone has had a chance to talk.
3. Stay on the topic. Follow the step-by-step directions.
4. Respect other class members. Use indoor voices.

1. Respect other group members. Listen to everyone's ideas.
2. Make decisions only after everyone has had a chance to talk.
3. Stay on the topic. Follow the step-by-step directions.
4. Respect other class members. Use indoor voices.

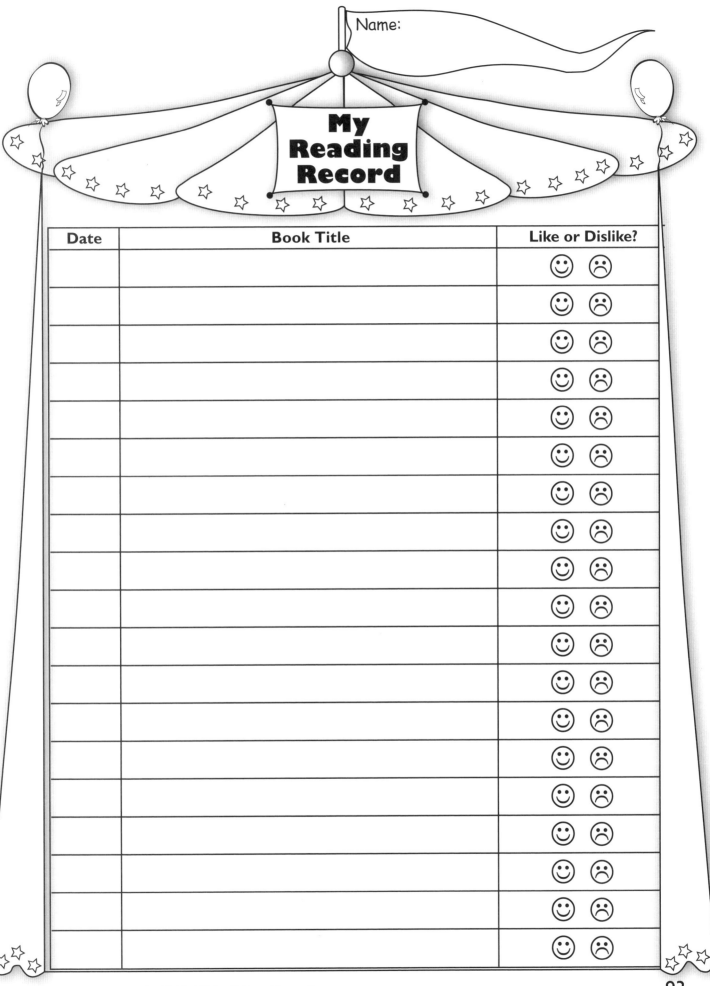

Name:

My Reading Record

Date	Book Title	Like or Dislike?
		☺ ☹
		☺ ☹
		☺ ☹
		☺ ☹
		☺ ☹
		☺ ☹
		☺ ☹
		☺ ☹
		☺ ☹
		☺ ☹
		☺ ☹
		☺ ☹
		☺ ☹
		☺ ☹
		☺ ☹
		☺ ☹
		☺ ☹
		☺ ☹
		☺ ☹
		☺ ☹

Name:

My Reading Record

Date	Book Title	Like or Dislike?
		☺ ☹
		☺ ☹
		☺ ☹
		☺ ☹
		☺ ☹
		☺ ☹
		☺ ☹
		☺ ☹
		☺ ☹
		☺ ☹
		☺ ☹
		☺ ☹
		☺ ☹
		☺ ☹
		☺ ☹
		☺ ☹
		☺ ☹
		☺ ☹

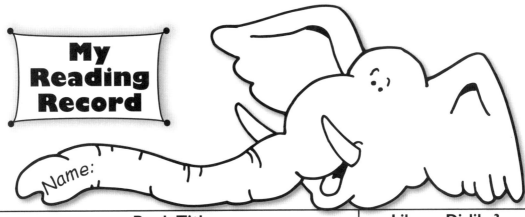

My Reading Record

Name:

Date	Book Title	Like or Dislike?
		☺ ☹
		☺ ☹
		☺ ☹
		☺ ☹
		☺ ☹
		☺ ☹
		☺ ☹
		☺ ☹
		☺ ☹
		☺ ☹
		☺ ☹
		☺ ☹
		☺ ☹
		☺ ☹
		☺ ☹
		☺ ☹
		☺ ☹
		☺ ☹

My Reading Record

Date	Book Title	Like or Dislike?
		☺ ☹
		☺ ☹
		☺ ☹
		☺ ☹
		☺ ☹
		☺ ☹
		☺ ☹
		☺ ☹
		☺ ☹
		☺ ☹
		☺ ☹
		☺ ☹
		☺ ☹
		☺ ☹
		☺ ☹
		☺ ☹
		☺ ☹
		☺ ☹

Name _____